Craven Creek

Craven Creek

A Collection of Essays

by

Walt Gasson

WordsWorth * Cody, Wyoming

Copyright © 2024 by Walt Gasson
All rights reserved. No part of this book may be reproduced in any manner without written permission from the publisher.

ISBN 978-1-7334897-3-7

First edition paperback

Cover photo by Andy Roosa.
Back cover photo of author by Andy Roosa.
Back cover photo of Old Walt from Gasson family archives.

Published by WordsWorth
Cody, Wyoming
WWW.WORDSWORTHPUBLISHING.COM

Printed in the United States of America

Contents

Foreword i
Introduction ii
Old Walt 5
Wapiti 11
Oregon Buttes 17
Harrie 23
Dinwoody 30
Requiem 40
Gus 47
Cutthroats 54
Haystacks Elegy 62
Grace 69
Farewell 78
B*ison bison* 83
The Home Place 92

Foreword

They come to me now, almost seven decades into my life. Unbidden but not unwelcome, the faces and the places of a life spent in Wyoming return to me in memory. I've tried to collect them here, not to preserve them like butterflies pinned to cardboard, but to share them. It's not that I think my life is especially unique. Many people have lived more interesting lives than I. But I think the act of telling these stories has value.

I have always loved hearing and telling stories. I grew up listening to the stories of men and women who were legitimate pioneers in a wild and forbidding place, the high deserts and mountains of western Wyoming. Those stories told by cowboys and sheepherders, miners and railroaders were the legends of our family, the underpinnings of a life lived in the Green River country. In time, I began to tell my own stories. I now tell them more often.

The title for this collection of stories comes from an insignificant little creek near the tiny community of Opal, Wyoming. Our family ranch straddled Craven Creek, and it was the headquarters for the Gasson family sheep outfit. Frankly, neither the creek nor the ranch was much of a going concern. Most of the year, the sheep were out on the range. Most of the year, Craven Creek ran only a trickle of water. There are thousands of creeks just like it across the American West.

And there are thousands of families just like ours out here on the sagebrush sea. Each is perhaps insignificant in itself. But taken collectively, we are the people of this hard country, western people, Wyoming people. We love this place. And when we get together at a birthday party or a branding or in an elk camp, we tell stories — stories like these.

Introduction

Our grandson Dillon was not quite 10 years old when he accompanied his uncle and his great uncle on one of those backcountry death marches that we sometimes undertake when we fish our home waters. They lost the trail somewhere above Big Sandy Lake and found themselves all boogered up in a deep canyon. They fought their way up the canyon wall through the rocks and deadfall and ended up at a spectacular cutthroat lake, just at timberline. The fishing was a little slow, so they struck out for another high-country lake and fished the afternoon away before they noticed it was almost dinner time and hoofed it back for the cabin. All told, they walked about 17 miles.

I thought it was admirable that our young grandson kept up all day long with the big guys—after all, not a lot of guys his age would walk 17 miles in one day under any circumstances. So, I told him how impressed I was with his grit. He said something that I can't forget: "Grandpa, that's just what we do in our family!"

And that got me thinking about what it is we do in our family. We don't have a family code or a mission statement or a sign over the door with an uplifting quote. But we have a firm knowledge of who we are and what we know to be true:

- **We love God.** We're not afraid to say that we're people of faith. I don't think we're pushy about it - we're too private for that. But our faith in the gospel of Jesus Christ strengthens us and sustains us through good times and bad times. We go to church on Sunday and try to live what we believe all week long.

- **We love one another.** We're a close family. We spend as much time together as we can. When one of us succeeds, we're all happy. When one of us is hurt, we all feel the pain. We've been through births and deaths and triumphs and tragedies together. Sometimes, it's been really hard, but we stick together.

- **We work hard.** My wife Kim's pet phrase, "He (or she) is a working machine," is the highest form of praise in our family. We build our own decks and make our own jelly. We start early and we don't quit until it's done. A thousand generations of German-Swiss farmer blood runs in our veins and we won't abide a slacker. In short, we're sorry you're tired but "Toughen up, Buttercup."

- **We value knowledge.** Some of us know Dickens and others know the law. Some of us can fix a chainsaw and others can make the best peach pie you ever ate. We read to our kids until they can read to us, and then we read together. We read a lot and we learn and grow all our lives.

- **We love wild things and wild country.** We're training the fifth generation of elk hunters in our outfit. We hunt on foot mostly, in places without roads and with few trails. We fish for cutthroats stocked by the Creator, not the creative. We cut our own firewood and our own Christmas trees. We know the lay of the land and the way it feels underfoot in every season of the year. We are as much a part of Wyoming as Wyoming is part of us.

We're not perfect. We know that. But we're trying to be a little bit better all the time. Sometimes we disagree, but we try to do that without hurting anyone. We try to work out our disagreements before they get too big. And in the end, we forgive one another and keep on keeping on. We never stop doing the things that make us who we are individually and who we are collectively as a family.

This book is for that family. And it's especially for the matriarch of that family, my beloved wife Kim.

Chapter 1

Old Walt

I never knew him. Never heard his voice or even saw his face, except in the old sepia-toned pictures that were handed down to me. My dad didn't remember him much, and I don't recall him ever mentioning his father to me. Never much of a mentioner to begin with, my father didn't have a lot of memories to work with when it came to his own father. Walter Fredrick Gasson was only 44 years old on January 13, 1920, when he died from pneumonia during the influenza pandemic. His son Henry Franklin Gasson was only 6.

Walt was born in Ogden, Yell Township, Boone County, Iowa on August 27, 1875. Ogden is near the center of Iowa, named for William B. Ogden, first mayor of Chicago and president of the Union Pacific Railroad. In 1875 Ogden was a farming community, a settled place a comfortable distance removed from the American frontier. The 1880 census recorded a population of 568. He was the first child born to Fredrick Gasson and Caroline Moerke. We have no pictures of him until 1885, when he was ten years old. He poses with his sisters Bertha and Ida and looks uncomfortable in front of the camera. In the next photo, taken in Green River in 1891, he's again posed with his sisters, and this time with his mother Caroline. Again, he looks uncomfortable. But he's 16 years old now and beginning to bear some resemblance to the man he would become. His gaze is direct, and his hands look strong.

Family lore says that he quit school in the fourth grade to help out on his father Fred's sheep ranch on Big Sandy Creek. The photographs are very scarce, and always taken out on the range. He's wearing a broad-brimmed, low crowned hat with a stampede strap,

Old Walt (L) on the range – Gasson Family Archives

beaded riding gloves (made by Dick Son's Shoshone wife out on Henry's Fork) and looking every inch the buckaroo. We have some indication that he was at Fred's place in 1895, when he found the body of a dead woman who drowned in the Green River near the mouth of Big Sandy Creek. But no other photos exist until after 1900.

In 1909, the best record of his life begins. He was 34 years old, and by his own description a "stockman." He was a member of the Masonic Lodge. He was a foreman for the big sheep outfit Gilligan and Franklin. And he carried a small pocket journal with him (compliments of the Rock Springs National Bank) in which he recorded the events of each day. He was in partnership with his brother-in-law Henry Franklin now, and he gave Henry's name as an emergency contact. He records that he is 5'5" tall and weighs 150 pounds. He wears a size 6⅞ hat, size 8½ gloves, size 15½ shirt, and size 6 boots. From the entries in in journal, terse though they are, he's clearly spending most of his time out with the sheep:

January 1, 1909. "Camped four miles west of Rock Springs."

March 29, 1909. "Forenoon nice. Afternoon snowed like hell, about 8 inches."

April 5, 1909. "Went to Dingle [Idaho]. Bought one mare. Snowed." He kept the bill of sale dated April 8, 1909. *"To whom it may concern: I this day sold to Gilligan and Franklin one light bay mare 6-year-old star in forehead left hind foot white. Branded FD in left thigh. Weight 1600. Theodore Dayton."*

July 21, 1909. "In Kemmerer. Sheep went on reserve." Walt had been dealing with the new U.S. Forest Service to move the Gilligan and Franklin sheep that had been grazing on the Bonneville Forest Reserve near Montpelier, Idaho to the Wyoming Forest Reserve near Cokeville. They wanted 2700, but the USFS would only allow 2400.

September 1, 1909. "Left our allotment. Feed all gone. Counted 2429." It was a short season on the forest reserve.

December 25, 1909. Walt had moved the sheep to a lease on some winter pasture near Rock Springs. *"Warmest day so far."* He didn't get a Christmas holiday.

They are short, laconic summaries of each day's events, never more than a few words and seldom relating to anything but the job at hand. Clearly, Walt is a guy who is working hard to be successful as a top hand for a big outfit. But changes are on the horizon. Henry Franklin married Walt's sister Ida (he was 43, she was 20) back in 1900. By 1909, Walt and Henry were looking for some opportunities of their own. On September 20, 1909, Henry wrote to tell Walt of the progress on the plan to buy out the Mallory Ranch on Craven Creek, east of Kemmerer, Wyoming. Things were looking up.

But there's also a letter dated November 8, 1909, from Henry. He had been to sell the sheep and came away deeply concerned. He didn't do well, and he notes his deeper concern about the scarcity of money and the banks closing. "The streets here have been and are now crowded with Henry's Forkers to get their money for their ranches. They have all sold from Phil Mass down to Dick Son." The financial panic of 1907 had come home to roost on Henry's Fork—a little too close to home perhaps for Henry. He was over 50 now, and he may have wanted to diversify, or he may have simply wanted to be in business with his wife and her brother. Whatever the reason, the place on Craven Creek became their joint venture.

And just in time, too. On February 28, 1911, Walt married Miss Harriet Heward of Evanston. Harrie (no one ever called her Harriet) was a teacher who taught in a host of small one-room schools in southwest Wyoming. The Green River Star reported, "Since the wedding, the happy couple have been enjoying a delightful trip on the Union Pacific lines, arriving in Green River today, where they will make their home. Mr. Gasson is a prominent sheep owner of this county, while the bride is a popular young lady of Evanston." He built his bride a home just west of the Sweetwater County Courthouse, and only a block from Henry and Ida's home in Green River.

In 1913, Walt noted that he was still employed by Gilligan and Franklin. But the daily notes are slightly different. Frequently, he just records "At ranch." He also seems to have landed a winter job with the City of Green River, but not for long. On March 22, 1913, his entry reads "Quit working for the city." By April 1 of that year, he's back on the range again. The semi-nomadic life of a stockman resumed:

April 2, 1913. "Went out to camp 2 mile below the Pilot Butte. Snowed and stormed."

June 29, 1913. "Rained. Moved into Dempsey Basin on the school section."

July 18, 1913. "Went over to Hobble Creek fishing. Poor luck—8 fish."

But on October 1, 1913, he waxed effusive: "Baby boy born yesterday. 3,543 in the herd. 81 black [sheep]." He must have been excited about the birth of Henry Franklin Gasson—the baby boy named for his much beloved partner and brother-in-law—but none of that makes it into his notes. He was at home from October 2 through October 6, but after a week he was back in Kemmerer and was on the ranch or out on the range until November 3. He's home again infrequently (but only passing through) until Christmas.

The records from the last five years of his life are few and far between. There's a warranty deed from 1915 in which James and Enger Chrisman sell him 164.2 acres in T. 22, R. 114 near Opal, in Lincoln County. There's a 1915 tax notice on that property and a separate one on another 330 acres in the same area. In the spring of 1916, there's a brand certificate when he registered his brand—the bench W—with the Board of Livestock Commissioners and a receipt from the store in Fossil, WY for supplies including eggs, salt, tobacco, syrup, and lard.

But in 1916, there would be another baby—a girl, named Caroline Claire. There are no records of his reaction to becoming a father again. But by 1918, there's a photo of him posing with his trombone in the Green River Band. Perhaps Harrie was successful in keeping him a little closer to home by then. If so, they were undoubtedly wonderful years, World War I notwithstanding. The war brought higher prices for wool and mutton, and the family prospered. But by 1918, the war in Europe had been replaced by war on the home front—an influenza pandemic.

In Wyoming, influenza wasn't reported until October 1918. It was almost certainly present before that. By 1919 its rapid spread outstripped the ability of the state's health care providers to deal with it. Public gatherings were canceled. People wore masks when in public, though these did little to prevent the spread of the disease. Influenza rates in Wyoming peaked in the fall of 1919, but the disease remained prevalent well into 1920.

Harrie and the children (Franklin, age 6 and Carol, age 3) had been with Walt at the ranch, but they all had moved to the house in Green River, perhaps so that Franklin could start school. Walt came to town for Christmas and stayed to ring in the new year. And somewhere in that stay, he contracted influenza. He grew sick at the ranch and had to be transported home. In death as in life, he didn't linger long at home.

The obituaries in the Green River Star and the Kemmerer Republican were short, but to the point. The Star notes that none but his closest friends knew the seriousness of his illness, and that only the previous Sunday he had been with his Masonic brethren conferring degrees of that order. The Republican says he had "recently removed from his ranch on Craven Creek near Kemmerer, leaving his place in the care of a caretaker, to Green River, to remain for the rest of the winter." He died on January 19, 1920, after an illness of 9 days, according to the death certificate signed by Dr. V.L. Looney. It lists the cause of death as "influenza, pneumonia" at age 44 years, 4 months, and 22 days.

Walt had gone home to stay.

Chapter 2

Wapiti

It is, to borrow a phrase from Cormac McCarthy, "no country for old men." The Wind River Range is a rock pile from South Pass to Togwotee Pass—it's hard on horses and harder on men. So it was, the morning we dropped down from the high meadows on the sheepherder trail and stopped for a snack and a drink of water. That's when we saw the elk. They were high, above timberline. We were sitting on a rock when they simply appeared out of nowhere a mile or more away, just little specks on a grassy shelf above a big rockslide. It was a good place to see a bighorn sheep, but it was full of elk: cows, calves, a couple of spikes and one monster of a bull. There was never any ques-

Bull Elk – Andy Roosa

tion about whether or not we would go after them. The only question was how, and that question was quickly put to rest as we made our way quickly to the cover of the timber.

It was a long approach, and a tough one. We moved up through a small meadow, staying in the cover of the scattered spruce at the edges. We slipped through the lower edges of the jumbled scree, boulder-hopping and keeping one eye above us to be sure we were below their line of sight. Then we were into the dense forest on the steep slope below them. We moved slowly, steadily up the slope until we ran out of timber, sweating, huffing and puffing, straining for each painful lungful of air.

Then we were naked, or at least it felt like we were. There were no trees, not even a bit of stunted fir. We stashed the daypacks, the jackets and everything else we didn't absolutely need. We were at almost 11,000 feet when we paused to catch our breath. That's when I saw her ears. One cow had risen from her bed and walked to the edge of the grassy shelf to look down the slope. There we were, without enough cover to hide a pika. We tried to huddle up and look like rocks, but she made us in one look. She barked once, wheeled on her hind legs and it was all over. We never even heard their footfalls, but we knew they were gone. We heard the big bull bugle one time in the timber below, and never saw him again.

Elk hunting is like real life—you have to learn to deal with disappointment. The plan was to hit the trail down in the bottom of the drainage and to drop down, maybe even head for the cabin. We were pretty well spent, and heartsick with defeat. But once we got into the timber, we began seeing elk tracks in the snow. A couple at first, then small bunches of a half dozen or so, all made that morning. All moving steadily, not hurrying, but not lingering in any one spot, either. And all headed in one direction.

Elk are creatures of habit in our part of the Wind Rivers, and these elk were starting the same journey they made every year at about this time. They would stay in the old growth timber and skirt the shoulder of the mountain well away from the trail in the bottom of the drainage. They would timber up for a night or two. Then, if the weather didn't clear up, they would move over into the next basin on their way to their winter range. Generations of them have successfully dodged Shoshone hunters, mountain men, tie hacks, my grandfather, and my father in this black timber tangle. And now it was my turn.

Lynn and James headed off down the drainage for the cabin, but I couldn't quite make myself quit hunting just yet. If I moved slowly and quietly, I could be in the meadow on the point of the mountain just at the witching hour—that magical time right around sunset when elk are most active. We have killed more of them in the last 30 minutes of daylight than in all the other hours of the day combined.

It had been a wonderful day. The disappointment of the failed sneak had disappeared. It was silent. It was still. It was perfect. There was a feeling that is difficult to explain, even when you have experienced it many times. The closest I can come is to borrow a term from baseball. Really good batters sometimes talk about being "in the zone." It's that flow state where your mind, your body and your spirit come together and focus completely. Everything slows down. Your mind is focused, with no thought of anything except the moment. Your body is loose, just tired enough to be content to move slowly, but fresh enough to keep up the pace for as long as it takes. And your spirit is one with the mountain. When everything is right and I'm "in the zone" like that, it's a feeling almost mystical in nature. I'm not invisible, but I'm not far from it.

It was almost mystical as well, the way I felt it coming that day. I knew without a doubt that it was going to happen soon, it was only a question of when. I eased forward one slow step at a time, feeling the ground with my feet to make sure I didn't make a noise. Slowly, quietly, carefully around the trees... I saw him at the exact instant that he saw me. One squeal and everything erupted into chaos! He seemed to go instantly from placidly standing broadside to full-tilt, all-out run. Things happened way too fast to think about them. At times like this, there is no real thinking. Your brain is simply processing information and you are reacting by instinct or else it's over. I remember thinking that he was a bull and a good one... that's all my brain registered. I don't remember raising the rifle, I don't even remember firing the shot, but I remember thinking "Yes! That one was good. That was a lung shot."

Mostly, I remember him. I remember how he watched me as he ran, not in fear but in calculated tactical retreat. I will never forget the feeling of watching his left eye as it clearly focused directly on me. I will take to my grave the way the muscles in his massive shoulders rolled and how his powerful hindquarters drove with each lunge, the way he sent great showers of snow and dirt up ten feet in the air behind him as he sprinted for the timber. The whole thing couldn't have taken more than a couple of seconds, but it all seems to slow down in my mind. I stood still and listened. I heard him go down in a shattering of branches behind a big granite boulder in the timber a couple hundred yards to my left. He tried to rise once, twice, and then lay still.

He was an old bull, gray in his mane and undoubtedly on the downhill side of his life. He was a good heavy six-point, but without the long tines he probably carried a couple of years ago. He had a bad gore wound between his shoulder and chest, and a collection of old scars from previous years' battles from the nape of his neck all the way to his rump. Three of his tines were broken. He was as thin as a snake. But he had been a brawler and a commanding presence on this mountain for years, only recently beginning to feel the onset of his old age. His teeth were worn, and he looked tired as he lay there. I sat beside him in the waning light of the afternoon and suddenly I was tired too. I felt a little on the downhill side of my years, too. I took the tenderloins for tomorrow night's dinner; made sure the tag was in his ear and headed for the trail as the last violet bit of alpenglow hung on the peaks behind me.

I broke into the big meadow above the the trailhead just as darkness fell. I sat on a rock and ate the last half of a bacon and cheese sandwich from my pack. I could just make out one of the folks from a camp on the far side as he walked four horses down to the creek to water. One was belled, and I could make out the sound, clear and pure in the gathering dim. I wondered how many times I'd been in this meadow at first light and last. I wondered how many times the bull had been, and if we'd seen one another before today. We might have been old friends, I thought as I got to my feet.

I knew someone would be waiting for me with a truck at the trailhead. Maybe it would be Kim. That would be good. There's no sweeter sight in the world than my wife's beautiful face at the end of a day like this. She has retired from hunting these elk, but she has run our elk camp flawlessly for decades. We live like royalty under her direction. Almost certainly Lynn would be there. Even if I didn't get there 'til midnight, he wouldn't worry. He would be there. No matter who it was, I'd be tired and happy to see them, because hunting has always been a family affair for us. Moms, dads, kids, and dogs—we all come to the home place to hunt elk. It's just what we do in our family. As I thought about it, I realized that our family isn't like most families—even in Wyoming.

That became clearer the next day. It turned out that the boys had killed a cow and calf not far from my bull on their hike back to the cabin. None of these elk were less than three and a half miles from the trailhead. The hunt was over and the packing had begun. The whole clan packed up and headed off up the trail. Six-month-old Connor went in a pack on his mother's shoulders, wearing a hunter orange cap and his first snowsuit. The rest of us carried backpacks for hauling out meat, hides and antlers.

We descended on those fallen elk and spent the morning skinning and butchering the cow and calf. We had them packed out in time to have lunch at the cabin. Then it was back up the trail again in the afternoon to skin and butcher the bull and pack out the meat. He was thin but still huge, and we had to leave enough meat for one more trip the following morning. It was hard work, and we all slept hard that night, even Connor.

The last trip up the mountain is always the hardest. I hurt from my neck to the soles of my feet from packing elk meat down the mountain. Lynn took the last pack full of meat, and I took the hide, skull, and antlers from the bull. The pack was heavy and so were my feet, but this is always a wonderful part of the hunt. The meat was in coolers. The hard work was almost over, and I could think as we moved slowly down off the mountain one last time. I thought about the bull. I thought about my good friend as he led the way down the trail. But mostly, I thought about my family and this place we love so much.

    I am older now, and I carry a lot of scars, just like that old bull. But I work hard to stay in shape for hunting far behind the "Road Closed to Motorized Travel" sign. I don't want an ATV, and I don't need one. I don't need the noise or the smell or the separation of my head and my heart from the land under my feet. But I do need this experience. I need to come with my family to the cabin in the fall when the aspens are gold. I need to get up in the dark and start the water heating and hear their sleepy voices. I need to be in the timber on the shoulder of the mountain when the sun comes up. And I need to feel that oneness of mind and body and spirit when I am alone on the mountain with the elk. I need these things as surely as my family needs that meat in the freezer.

    For all of us, that meat and this experience will feed us, both physically and spiritually, during the coming months. And that will make us the people we are as individuals and the family we are together.

Portions of this essay appeared in the December 2002 issue of Wyoming Wildlife magazine.

Chapter 3

Oregon Buttes

They rise like battlements out of the vast sagebrush sea. The buttes and desert peaks of our homeland are the harder country in the middle of the hard country. The old-timers steered by these landmarks in the days before maps on your phone, or even maps folded up haphazardly on your dashboard. The roads were few and far between back then. So were people. Only a few of my dad's old desert rat buddies even knew some of those places existed. But those places left a mark on me, one that remains to this day. I grew up loving the taste of young sage grouse. I can see an antelope a very long way off, and I

Oregon Buttes – Andy Roosa

can tell if it's a buck without binoculars, just by the way he moves. I feel crowded if I can see someone else, even if they're a mile away. I even like wild horses—up to a point. Not very many people knew the desert when it was wild and fewer of them ever loved it. I did, and I still do.

I don't remember the first time I went to the Jack Morrow Hills country. Maybe that's because there were no "Jack Morrow Hills" then. That isn't to say that my first trip to the country happened while it was still a shallow, inland sea. It is to say, though, that for those of us who grew up in the country the term "Jack Morrow Hills" was simply never used. There was Jack Morrow Creek, just as there was Pacific Creek or Bear Creek or Killpecker Creek. There was Joe Hay Rim, Oregon Buttes and Steamboat Mountain. But I never heard anyone refer to anything in that part of the country as "hills." Hills are tame places, not wild country like this. Hills are gentle, green slopes with flowers, grass, and butterflies. It wasn't like that out here. The northern Red Desert country was a wild place, and that's how I remember it. That's how I fell in love with it.

I remember getting up long before daylight, when the nights were just beginning to turn cool in late summer. I remember the smell of coffee from his thermos and the green glow from the dashboard of the pickup on his face as my dad and I headed out into the night. The moon was still out as we drove through Rock Springs and up the highway past Reliance. By the time the sun came up, we were north of Steamboat Mountain. The roads weren't good then, and there weren't a lot of them. They were rough and rutted. Sometimes the creek crossings were washed out after a rain, and even a short cloudburst could turn them into greasy gumbo mud. But we had shovels, tire chains, two spare tires and lots of food and drinking water. The desert kept a hard school, but it was my father's alma mater. When the sunrise came to the sea of gray sagebrush, it was like no place on earth.

There were sage grouse in the country then, but they were still called sage chickens. And there were a lot of them. In southwestern Wyoming, the opening day of sage chicken season was, to a 10-year-old boy in the mid-1960s, at least as good as Christmas. It might have been as good as Christmas, my birthday, and Easter all rolled up in one. It was the first hunt of the year, usually in late August. We hunted in the early morning when the birds were moving to and from water. It's cool at that time of day in the desert, and the smell of the sagebrush was intoxicating. The excitement of the first hunt of the season was like fire in my soul. I walked along with the old man as he flushed covey after covey of birds. Sometimes he'd just watch the birds fly, never even raising the old Model 12. Other times, he'd pick a young bird out of the bunch and down it with a single shot. I don't remember him ever missing. I got to carry the empty shotshell hulls. I still remember the smell of gunpowder from the spent casings. I got to hold the dead birds, too, warm in my hand. We'd see maybe 200 or 300 birds on a good day in those years. It's hard to see more than two or three bunches now.

Not all our trips were hunting trips. The old man liked to go to Oregon Buttes just about any time of year. We'd have lunch in a little aspen grove on the west side of the buttes and then just go poke around to see what we'd find. He'd tell me about the old-time sheep and cattle outfits in the country. He'd tell me about his family and their outfit over on Craven Creek. My dad, Gus, had deep roots in the desert country. He'd point out the peaks of the Wind Rivers to the north, the Wyoming Range to the west, even Pine Mountain clear down on the Colorado border to the south. The desert air was cleaner then, and you could see forever.

Sometimes, we'd gather up cones from the limber pines and put them in gunnysacks to take home. The old man would soak them in various chemicals he bought at the Rexall Drug in Green River to make them burn in a rainbow of color when we tossed them in the fireplace at the cabin. I expect that if you tried to buy the same chemicals today, there'd be Homeland Security agents on your doorstep the next morning. We weren't that paranoid then, Cold War or not.

One time, we were headed up the west side of the north butte, and the old man was far in the lead. My legs were a good bit shorter then, and I was huffing and puffing as I brought up the rear. When I finally caught up with him, he was puzzled. He had just seen a small mammal unlike anything we'd ever seen before in our part of the country. It wasn't a weasel, but it was sort of weasel shaped. It wasn't a raccoon, but it had rings on its tail. We went home and looked through the field guide, finally concluding that it was a ringtail (*Bassaricus astutus*). These members of the raccoon family are common in Utah and Arizona, but way out of their element this far north in Wyoming. What the poor ringtail was doing on Oregon Buttes is still beyond me, but he and Gus met pretty much eyeball to eyeball, and it was hard to tell who was more surprised.

Ringtails aside, this is a biodiversity hotspot. There are plants and animals here that live no place else in Wyoming. I'm not a good enough botanist to know most of them, but I know the basin big sagebrush communities in the country that grow higher than my head. Some of those sagebrush plants were here when my great-grandfather came out here from Iowa to take up a place on Big Sandy Creek. Old-growth sagebrush, if you will, it has stems as big around as your arm. It's the tallest thing that grows for miles in any direction. Old Fred Gasson was a sheepman, and I doubt he paid the slightest attention to the large-fruited bladderpod, intermountain phacelia, compact gilia or any of the other unique plants out here, but for plant geeks like me they're pretty darn cool.

So are the Killpecker Dunes. A vast sea of shifting sands, they look like a scene from Lawrence of Arabia. Not much grows there, but the things buried within them can be rare indeed. When he was a young man, my father found a complete fossilized turtle skeleton in the dunes one day. At that time, he wanted to be an archaeologist or maybe a paleontologist, so he telephoned the University of Wyoming museum to tell them about it. They asked him to send it to them. He did, but without much in the way of careful padding. By the time it arrived in Laramie, it was a box of rubble. The whole paleontologist thing pretty much went to rubble itself later on. Old Gus dropped out of the university to come home to Green River just in time to be swept up in World War II. He was lucky to come home from the South Pacific, but the scars remained his whole life.

For me, I love the little seeps and springs, the fragile tendrils of green that wind through the monochrome of gray sagebrush in the Jack Morrow country. These muddy little waterholes and miniature streams are the arteries that support life in the desert. If you fly over this wild country at 30,000 feet, especially in the late summer, it's rough and gray-brown like the hide of some enormous beast. But those little green tendrils stand out. Tiny little seeps bubble up from deep in the earth and make up the capillaries that feed the larger gullies to form the veins and arteries—the circulatory system that sustains this harsh landscape.

They have sustained it for time out of mind. From the first people living in pit houses, hunting and gathering to make a living, to the Shoshone people who knew every inch of it, people have been on this land for a long time. It's easy to feel a kinship with them when you take the time there to shed the layers of twenty-first century living. You feel them there, with the elk and the antelope and the spirits of the long-gone buffalo. If you just sit quietly and alone, you can still feel the magic of the place. You feel it in the silence, in the night so dark you can see the stars from horizon to horizon. You feel it in the chill of the sunrise, and in the great emptiness as it is revealed by the morning light.

I took my friend Lynn elk hunting there years ago, when he was in a residency program for family practice doctors in a major metropolitan area of the Midwest. We sat on a rim near Essex Mountain one day and ate lunch. We could see all the way to the Haystacks, south of Wamsutter. We could see the Uintas in Utah, and the Wyoming Range west of Big Piney. And we couldn't see a single sign of a human in any direction. He looked at it in silence for a while, and then said, "If you could see this far where I live—you can't, but if you could see this much country—there would be over 10 million people living in it."

The magic of the desert country is in its great loneliness. It is the great, silent emptiness of the place that has drawn us there for years. It is the chance to feel small in the overwhelming scope of the land. Those of us who have always known it have probably taken that quality for granted. But how many places are there in America where you can still feel this small? Feeling small is humbling, and 21st century Americans struggle to find humility. But I wonder sometimes if an occasional reminder of our own insignificance might not be just what we need.

Portions of this essay appeared in the July 2003 issue of Wyoming Wildlife magazine.

Chapter 4

Harrie

I knew her and loved her from the time of my birth in 1954 to the time of her death in 1969. I say that, but looking back, I wonder if I knew her at all, or if I knew the real Harriet Heward Gasson. It's not that I remember my paternal grandmother as angry or cantankerous in any way; I just don't remember her being happy. I think she was at one time, but I think that time was long before my time. I wish I had known her when she was younger—when she was happy.

My father's mother Harriet Ann Heward was born in Hucknall in Nottinghamshire in 1880 to Laban and Elizabeth Fearn Heward. Hucknall is in central England, and at the time was a coal mining center. From 1295 until 1915, the town was known as Hucknall Torkard, taken from Torcard, the name of a dominant landowning family. During the 19th and 20th centuries, coal was discovered and mined heavily throughout the area. Laban was a coal miner. Harriet was a coal miner's daughter.

"Harrie" immigrated to the United States as a small child on a ship loaded with English converts to the Church of Jesus Christ of Latter-Day Saints. One can only imagine that Laban, a stern Presbyterian lay minister, might have been a little uncomfortable when they offered him a Book of Mormon. The family settled in Almy, near Evanston, Uinta County, Wyoming where Laban found work in the mines that supplied coal to the Union Pacific Railroad. The Heward family grew to include eight children: Mary Jane (b.1876), Arthur (b.1877), Harriet (b.1880), Selina (b.1882), Harold (b.1883), Clara (b.1886), Ethel (b.1889) and Clarence Ernest (b.1893). Another daughter was born and died in 1896. Her mother Elizabeth died the same year.

Almy was a dangerous place for a coal miner. Late the night of January 12, 1881, an explosion killed 38 miners in the Central Pacific Mine. The mine had been troubled with gas for some time before the explosion. Another explosion killed 13 miners in 1886, and a third explosion in nearby Red Canyon in 1895 killed 62 miners, the third worst mining disaster in Wyoming history. Following the second explosion, the Wyoming legislature established the office of the state mining inspector, which subsequently shut down the Almy mines in the 1940s after it was deemed too dangerous to mine there.

By 1895, Harrie was 15 years old and well on her way to being a high school graduate. She was a tall, dark-haired pretty girl. A photo of the family taken at about that time shows her with her seven siblings and her father. Her hair is upswept in the style of the day, and she wears a high collared white blouse with a locket. She looks shy. But looks can be deceiving, and upon graduating from high school she qualified to be a teacher. One can only imagine that any young woman willing to teach the offspring of ranchers, railroaders, and miners in places like Evanston, Kemmerer and Diamondville must have been made of stern stuff indeed.

I never remember my grandmother speaking of her teaching experiences, but she must have enjoyed them. In that place and time, she was considered a career woman. We have no record of her life, not even much in the way of photographs, until she married my grandfather, Walter Fredrick Gasson, in Evanston on February 28, 1911. He was 36, she was 30. The Green River Star reported the news, referring to her as "a popular young lady of Evanston" and to Walt as "a prominent sheep owner of this county."

Even in the florid prose of the day, that's probably a whopper of an overstatement. Mr. Gasson was certainly a sheep owner, but one who was just a bit above sheepherder and significantly below any kind of prominence. Still, they had plans for their outfit and neither of them was any stranger to hard work. But Walt was still a hired hand, riding for the outfit owned in part by his brother-in-law Henry Franklin and his sister Ida Franklin Gasson. The Gilligan and Franklin brand was painted on sheep scattered over much of southwestern Wyoming, and

HARRIE

Walt and Harrie – Gasson Family Archives

Walt had been a top hand. He was in the saddle nearly every day of the year — checking camps, hiring and firing herders and making sure the sheep were well cared for in the hard high desert country.

But he must have been home sometimes, because two years later Harrie was expecting a baby. She was never at home on the range, and Walt had built her a handsome home on a corner lot in Green River. He had even tried working in town for a short period, but it was no good. He was happy to be home when he was home, but his life was out on the sagebrush sea with the sheep. He came in only for short periods. He was home on September 30, 1913, when Harrie gave birth to their son Henry Franklin Gasson.

Three years later, a daughter came into their lives—a beautiful dark-haired girl who they named Caroline, after Walt's mother.

Harrie had divided her time between the ranch they had purchased on Craven Creek north of Opal and the house in town. With two children now, time with Walt at the ranch was wonderful but it was clear that the house in Green River would be their home. The ranch was an outpost, an island of home in the high desert country.

Harrie told wonderful stories about the ranch. She remembered sage grouse by the hundreds along the little creek. She told of accompanying Walt when he hunted them and laughed at the memory of pointing the shotgun first at one rising bird and then another, but never managing to fire at them. Still, he must have fired a number of times, since she remarked that it didn't take long to fill a wagon bed with dead grouse.

The ranch prospered, and so did the Gassons. Wool and mutton prices were riding high through the years of World War I. Harrie and Walt went on trips in the new Studebaker touring car with Henry and Ida, the ladies dressed up fancy in big hats and dresses. The future looked bright and the children were thriving. Then, on January 19, 1920, the last gasp of the great influenza pandemic in Lincoln County took the life of Walt Gasson. He was only 44, and it was the darkest day of her life.

The ranch was sold to the Taliaferros of Green River Livestock, and Harrie and the kids moved to town permanently. She couldn't impose on Henry and Ida, and taking up a job teaching with two preschoolers of her own wasn't an option. So she took in boarders. Green River was first and foremost a railroad town, with men who needed a place to sleep and board between their shifts on the Union Pacific. Harrie had a big home, and she could cook.

Soon (perhaps too soon, as I suspect the gossips of this little railroad town observed) one of these boarders took a shine to this attractive widow. His name was William Bovee, and he was from Nebraska. For a lonely woman with limited ability to support her young family, his attention was welcome. But let us be clear. Harrie was the daughter of stern old Laban Heward and she had no illusions about what constituted proper conduct. Bovee asked for her hand in marriage, and she accepted. She bought a wedding dress and he returned to Nebraska to settle his affairs so that he could take up a new life in Green River with his ready-made family. He may have been preoccupied with thoughts of that new life when he started a fire in the woodstove with gasoline, rather than the usual kerosene. The ensuing explosion and fire killed him instantly. In less than a year, Harrie lost the only two men she would ever love. She was devastated.

No one in our family ever talked about Bovee. I didn't even know of his existence, much less his love or his tragic death, until long after my grandma was gone. Gassons are infamous for simply not talking about some things. But I think we may be similarly infamous for facing hardships with heads down and teeth gritted, willing to just tough it out. And so she did. I think she may have checked out of motherhood for a while, finding it just too hard to bear. Franklin (later nicknamed Gus) and Caroline (soon shortened to Carol) were raised by their aunt and uncle. Henry and Ida had no children of their own, they were well-fixed financially, and they loved the two little ones with all their hearts.

Harrie just did the best she could—a hallmark of women in the high desert country from time out of mind, and just the same today. She was a widow, and she was done being anything else. She was close to her family in Evanston, her brothers Harold and Ernest and especially her sister Ethel. She went to Evanston often, sometimes with the children, sometimes alone. She was good at being alone. Let Auntie and Uncle take the kids. She would be alone.

In time, she cultivated the friendships of other women her age, many of them widows of the pioneer stockmen of the Green River country. Mrs. Tinker, Mrs. Pearson, Mrs. Brinegar—I suspect these women may have had first names, but my father and his sister never referred to them in such a familiar way. Even my grandma called them primarily by their last names, omitting the "Mrs." as a nod to her close friendship with them. They drank tea and played euchre and enjoyed a respite, I suspect, from being the formidable queens of their respective tribes. They wore flowered dresses and hats and carried pocketbooks but wore the hard experiences of their years with a shared dignity.

The children grew up, as children mostly do. Both were dark-haired and handsome. Their senior pictures show them looking a good deal like their Heward grandmother, the strikingly beautiful Lizzie Fearn. But they were far from being just slick looking town kids. Both were tutored in the outdoor school of Ida Gasson Franklin, and they could skin a coyote and cook over a juniper fire with the rest of the tough ranch kids in Sweetwater County. Like all parents, Harrie must have looked on in wonder sometimes at her offspring and wondered where they came from.

They grew up and she grew old, there in the house on the corner across from the old courthouse. Carol married Grant Morck, a poor Norwegian kid who was a good enough baseball player to get a tryout with a big league team but came back to Green River because he was homesick. Gus went off to the University of Wyoming, the first Gasson to do that. Ida paid the bills on that ill-founded adventure. In two years, he was back home again. Carol and Grant moved in downstairs and life went on. Harrie was there to see Gus off when his National Guard unit was called off to fight in the South Pacific, and she was there when he came home a wreck. She was there as Carol repeatedly tried to launch a career in motherhood and failed. Long gone was the light-hearted young Harrie of her first three decades, replaced by the no-nonsense middle-aged matriarch.

When Gus drank too much for too long, she threatened to have him committed to the state mental hospital. When Carol went to work in the bank, I'm sure she raised one eyebrow in skepticism but came to see it as a good thing. And the years went by. Gus dried out and married Grace Gravelle the librarian, to the surprise of everyone — including the bride and groom. Carol and Grant moved upstairs in the big house to help Harrie. She was gracious about it, but it signaled the state of things to come. Her raven hair was white now, and she moved slower. She became a grandmother at the age of seventy-four.

She must have been happy to see me. Maybe she saw early on the similarities between old Walt and young Walt, the strapping little boy and the long-dead love of her life. She must have recognized the fascination with horses and guns and dogs as a shadow of the man who took her to the country dances a half-century ago, then vanished off with the sheep for weeks at a time. She didn't mind when I wore my six-shooters to the Sunday dinner table. She drew the line at roping in her dining room, but sent me outside with a slice of homemade bread instead of a scolding. We understood each other, my grandma and me. She was long gone before I understood that connection.

She grew more and more rickety as time went on, and when she broke a hip while visiting Aunt Ethel's place on Bear River, it was the beginning of the end. She struggled to recover and spent most of her time in her chair with her feet up. She occupied the corner bedroom at Carol and Grant's new home across from the high school, and it was there she received the grim news of her son's death from a heart attack at age 53. No mother expects to outlive her son, and it must have been like a knife in her heart. But I do not remember her crying. She simply did what she always did when faced with a tragedy — she endured. Doggedly, sternly, stubbornly — she endured.

She did not endure for long. A few years later, Harrie was gone. I was a high school sophomore, and uncomfortable when I could not summon tears at her funeral. I wondered what was wrong with me, that I could not grieve for this stern old woman who had meant so much in my life. Now I know that I was just doing what she taught me to do, to do the same thing she had done and what her mother and father had done before her. Much like the sagebrush sea that has been our home, we endure.

Chapter 5

Dinwoody

There is a time-honored joke among horsemen about the reason the Nez Perce people rode Appaloosa horses into battle. According to the old packers, these flashy spotted horses were universally so stupid and ornery that riding them ensured that the warriors would be in a towering rage when they got there. Mud was an Appaloosa, and he belonged to my old friend Tory. He took me most of the way to our sheep hunting camp. He was medium-sized, with a few scattered white spots and a stubborn streak. Tory loved him, and that made one of us.

Mud puffed out his belly when we saddled him that bright fall morning, so the cinch would be loose when I climbed aboard. That

High country bighorn – Andy Roosa

was my first clue. The old cowboys say that you can tell a lot about a horse by simply looking into his or her eyes. When I halted to re-tighten the cinch, I looked into Mud's eyes and all I saw was deceit. I completely missed the malice, contempt, and the disregard for all things human. I don't mean to say he was a bad horse. Wait...no, actually I do. Mud and I started out from the trailhead knowing that he would give me hell before the day was over. He did.

It was an epic ride up the old trail up Vomit Hill, over Arrow Mountain, across Burro Flat and down through the rockslides back into the timber on Dinwoody Creek. If I hadn't been so tired, it would have been awe-inspiring. The Dinwoody runs fast and deep through spruce and fir in its canyon. Gannett Peak looms to the west with the Dinwoody Glacier so close you can feel the wind off the ice. As it was, it was about 4 PM and I was dead tired. My backside was raw, and my legs were just about done for the day. Mud was a veteran of many long trails, and he knew by the way I sat the saddle that I was ready to be tried. It happened just above Clay Voss' old camp on Downs Fork. I stopped to stretch my legs, and when I started to mount him for the last two miles of the twenty we would ride that day, Mud exploded.

My left foot was in the stirrup and I was clinging to the saddle horn with my left hand. I was trying desperately to turn his head with the reins in my right, all the while hollering "Whoa, you miserable SOB! Whoa!" What I remember most was the way the trees went by in slow motion, like things do in a major horse wreck. I kept thinking about all those sharp stobs on the trees and logs and hoping I wouldn't be impaled on any of them.

We flew past Lynn and Tory, stopping to touch the ground only when old Mud needed solid footing for a boost into the air again. At some point, I came to rest on my face, but still clutching the reins. Mud stood over me, wild-eyed and blowing. Lynn rode up and said, "If I'd known you were gonna do that, I would have had the camera ready!" I rode that miserable little horse the rest of the way to our camp, just to show him that he couldn't intimidate me, but I never rode him again. When Tory took him home the next morning, I wished them both a good day. But I secretly hoped Mud would be take-out lunch for a grizzly bear.

Our camp was on Downs Fork, just below the mouth of Grasshopper Creek. Downs Fork is loud and fast, a happy little creek. It makes you smile just to listen to it—sort of like underwater zydeco. You can hear rocks rolling and crashing and the water on stone as old as the earth. It's an unearthly greenish white color, laden with glacial silt below Gardner Glacier, clear as Irish crystal above it. Anyplace there isn't a lake to catch the glacial silt, the streams around here carry a load of ground granite.

Camp was a simple affair, a small backpacking tent with sleeping pads and bags inside, a small fire ring and cooking gear some distance away, with groceries suspended fifteen feet off the ground some distance from that. Bears are a thing in the Dinwoody country, and nobody likes midnight visitors that weigh 400 pounds and may mistake you and your sleeping bag for a super-size burrito. Hence, anything that might smell like food is kept near the kitchen, not in the bedroom. There were few grizzlies in the Dinwoody at that time, but having a black bear come visit your tent is no great blessing.

Sheep hunting in the Wind Rivers is both agony and ecstasy. It is the tortuous search for an incredibly elusive quarry in sheer granite cliffs and thousand-foot avalanche chutes in a country that is as fresh and wild as it was when creation's first dew was still on it. It requires climbing at least 1,500 vertical feet every day in heart-pounding pulls where your legs scream for a stop and there isn't enough air to fill your lungs and you taste blood every time you swallow. It requires sitting for hours motionless while you search every square inch of a ridge with a spotting scope that threatens to suck the eyeballs right out of your head. Your head aches and you're hungry all the time and your legs and feet hurt and you're either too hot or too cold, but you love it. Most importantly, it requires that you make peace with the mountain.

The mountain is an overwhelming presence in sheep country. I don't mean a specific mountain or even a specific place. More like a combination of forces like cold, wind, ice, altitude, and slippery rock that serve to remind you of how fragile you really are. You can come to the mountain, even spend some time there and grow to love it. But you cannot take it for granted. If you do, you find yourself looking down a 1,500-foot chasm in a hurricane snowstorm with no earthly idea where you are or how you will live to tell about it.

Goat Flat is a place like that. It is the eeriest place I have ever been. Graded flat as a pool table by the great glaciers millions of years ago, it lies at 12,000 feet above sea level between Downs Fork, Dinwoody Creek and Bomber Creek, inaccessible without a heartbreaking climb. It's a wind-blasted jumble of razor-sharp rocks and blasted out barrens. There's sheep sign and a bird flies by once in a while, but mostly, there's just wind and rock and snow.

You hear voices in the wind sometimes and they shriek and howl in your ears. Every place has a spirit, and the spirit of Goat Flat is tortured. Nothing grows over two inches tall there, and life clings precariously to a tiny mouthful of soil that holds a tiny mouthful of grass. It reminds me of the Barrow Downs in Tolkien's *Lord of the Rings*, where Frodo encounters the spirits of long-dead warriors. I wouldn't want to be there at night.

But sheep live there, taking the tiny mouthfuls of grass, leaving small strings of marble-sized turds and living their lives pretty much as their ancestors did before men ever came to the Wind River country. Gray-brown bodies with bright white rumps and deep amber eyes too large for the rest of their heads, they eat and drink, mate, and fight like they have here since they came south down the Rocky Mountain chain before the big ice sheet.

The ewes look small and frail, with spindly legs and a curious streak. The lambs are like all other children of wild mammals, preoccupied with food and play, now venturing forth, now hiding behind their mothers. They run and tumble like kittens but think nothing of bailing headlong off a thirty-foot cliff, bouncing occasionally to slow their descent and landing on their feet like cats.

But the rams, oh the rams—they are like nothing else I know on this earth. Short-coupled and blocky, built like brick outhouses, they lie in the sun on a warm fall day and survey everything below them with binocular eyes. They are big and strong and they reek of arrogance. They rise slowly, heaving their bulk up and turning the heavy, sweeping curl of their horns to look, smell and listen before they move. In a land of no visible cover, they can disappear mystically and completely just by standing still. They are mythic creatures, the stuff of firelight tales since there have been sheep hunters to pursue them.

I am no great sheep hunter. Sheep hunting came too late to me, and my knees are too decrepit to take me to the places I would need to go to be a great sheep hunter. I learned too late in life what real sheep hunters have always known, from the Mountain Shoshones who herded them into rock corral traps to Jack O'Connor and my old friend Steve Kilpatrick, that sheep are to hunting what calculus is to arithmetic. Sheep hunting is a soaring of the spirit, a lifting of the heart and a chance to know in every molecule of your being that wildness is the most precious thing left on earth. It is that wildness that draws us to sheep hunting as surely as the tender young grass shoots draw the sheep themselves.

We rose every morning before light and ate our oatmeal by the tiny fire in the half light of the canyon. We shouldered our packs and tightened our boots and climbed, sweating and straining, to the little pockets between Klondike and Grasshopper Creeks, to the big slopes on Downs Lake or to the cliffs above unnamed glacial pools on the top of the world. We moved along carefully, just below the ridgelines so as never to skyline ourselves, until we found some vantage point from which to glass.

"Glass" is a verb in the vernacular of sheep hunting. It means to use your binoculars first, then your spotting scope to minutely examine every square inch of a mostly vertical piece of real estate that might be as big as most counties in Indiana. You sweep it slowly and carefully with the binocs first, never looking for a whole sheep, just a visual cue: a butt, a nose, any form of movement, anything that doesn't fit. Then you begin the brain-bending process of using the spotting scope to examine every bit of it. You start up close and move farther away. You scan first horizontally and then vertically, stopping with every new field of view to concentrate on each rock or stunted fir that might provide a windbreak for a bedded ram. You repeat this process for hours, and it becomes tedious, tortuous work. Your head aches and your eyes get red and bloodshot. You have to mentally force yourself to stay in each place and glass when all your instincts say, "Let's move. There's nothing here. I'm bored. Let's go. Now!" Then, when you can stand it no longer, you move to another vantage point that might be 100 yards or 10 miles away and repeat the process.

Occasionally, you stop to eat or drink. The first few days, you're hungry a lot. Then you get used to going without food and your stomach shrinks into a hard little ball that gets full on a package or two of instant oatmeal or some cheese and crackers and a protein bar.

But you still get thirsty. Really thirsty. And you must drink – even before you get thirsty. You make yourself drink, because you can do without food, but you cannot keep up this level of exertion without water. You filter water from the creeks, you filter water from the lakes. You filter water from little rock pools with bugs and sheep turds in them and hope for the best. But you drink a lot. And sometimes you worry about giardia. Nasty little microbes that are spread by lots of different critters, they get in the water and then they get in you. They make you violently ill, with days of vomiting and diarrhea that help you lose those ten pounds you don't want and another thirty to go with them. But the good news is that it won't affect you for another two weeks, so you drink anyway. And you keep glassing, and you keep walking, and you keep hunting.

Sometimes you get in trouble. We got in trouble one afternoon over in Sheep Heaven. That's the name we gave to a long series of small, protected pockets on the ridge between the Clear Fork of Grasshopper Creek and Klondike Creek. We spent all of one morning there, and it was more than worth the climb. It was perfect. It was completely hidden, and almost inaccessible to anybody but a sheep. There was lots of grass, there was water and there was sheep sign everywhere. It even smelled like sheep.

We jumped a small bunch of ewes and lambs out of their beds immediately. We sat down and glassed quietly for an hour or so, had a meager lunch and a rest, then began to move slowly and quietly from one pocket to the next. We tiptoed, we slunk, and we concentrated intently on finding a ram. There simply had to be one there. We saw ram tracks — fresh ones. We found beds and places where they had fed. But we didn't find a ram. Then, about mid-afternoon, the temperature began to drop and the wind picked up. I put on my vest, then my fleece jacket, then my windproof shell. And once, when I looked up, I saw the storm.

It was moving in fast from the west. It obliterated Gannett Peak, then moved down into Dinwoody, Klondike and Grasshopper. In a few minutes, it was sleeting, then snowing. In less time than that, you couldn't see fifty feet. We tried to get down off the exposed ridge in the direction of the Clear Fork. Moving slowly, we looked for an avalanche chute we had seen a couple of days before from below. Lynn went first in case we jumped a ram out of the maelstrom. Sometimes I could see him, sometimes I couldn't. Then, dimly I saw him stop short and freeze. I thought he saw a sheep, so I moved up slowly behind him.

"What?" I whispered.

"Look down," he said. The next step in front of him was 800 feet below in a scree slope. I felt sick. We worked our way very carefully back away from the edge and paralleled it until we found a way to crabwalk our way down through the ice-coated rocks. Slick, treacherous, and sharp as razors, they scared me. Visions of compound fractures danced in my head and all thoughts of sheep left me until we dropped out of the blizzard into the rain in a little grassy pocket that led back to the Downs Fork. I asked Lynn if he wanted to hunt some more before it got dark. Soaking wet and cold and bedraggled and scared, he said, "No. It's time to quit hunting and start surviving."

But sheep hunting is not made up entirely of lung-busting work, tedious glassing, and brutal weather. It's also made up of turquoise lakes, pink snow on the glaciers and slopes of wildflowers. There are pikas in the rockslides, like oversized hamsters with little innocent rabbit faces, too clueless to recognize you as a potential predator. There are mama moose with their homely calves feeding in the creek bottom and looking at you like they've never seen a human being before. Maybe they haven't. There is the sheer immensity of the country — intimidating sometimes, but incredibly exhilarating.

And there is the feeling of being closer to the spirit of the wilderness than you've ever been in your life. You camp in the same trees where the Tukudika camped, and the First People before them. You sit by your fire before you lay your tired body down for the night in your warm sleeping bag and you watch the same stars that Ned Frost watched, that John Colter watched, that Washakie watched, that those first people watched. And you shake your head in the sheer mystical wonder of it all.

On the last morning, we packed up our camp, shouldered our packs and began the climb up to Goat Flat one last time. It was hard. I was tired, and the pack was heavy. We took a long time inching our way up the ridge above Hell Gulch onto the flat, and when we got there, I was ready to quit. But we pressed on. First by line of sight and then by compass reading, we boulder-hopped and hunted our way across the next eight miles. It took all day, and we only stopped for drinks and a snack or two. We had just enough food to carry us out. By late afternoon, we were exhausted. My knees were swollen and each jump was a separate agony. Then I looked up and saw a storm coming down the Dinwoody that looked like the finger of God.

It hit suddenly, on the wings of a screaming west wind. Suddenly, it was half-light and then there was a blizzard. We could see Burro Flat from where we were, but it took until after dark to get down there. Lynn fell once, but he got back up and kept going. He has always been much faster than I on the downhills and over the boulders. We were both soaking wet and freezing by the time we made it to the little stand of subalpine fir above the trail.

We got the tent up and ate a quick and silent supper under a jury-rigged rain fly. I don't remember what it was, but it was hot and it was good and I was thankful for a best friend who can cook in a snowstorm. We were soon in our bags in the tent, shivering to warm the cocoon of air inside. It was hard to sleep, and I did so restlessly as the wind howled and the snow pelted our little camp. My knees and shoulders and back hurt, and the inside of my sleeping bag smelled like unwashed humanity. But in the end, I was too tired to hurt or to care anymore and I slept.

We walked out the next day to the trailhead in a whiteout blizzard down to about 9,000 feet. I slipped and fell to my knees once, and to this day Lynn swears I was praying that the snow would stop. Sure enough, the drizzling rain kicked in at about 8,000 feet and somewhere below that we found a lovely Indian summer afternoon. We glassed where we could, mostly to give ourselves the illusion of hunting, but we were done in. By the time we could see the truck, I was grateful that I didn't have another pair of socks to carry out, much less a ram. But if he'd seen one, he'd have killed it and I'd have packed it — somehow.

I look back on it now as the best of a zillion hunts in many respects. We never killed a ram in ten days in the upper Downs Fork country that year. I wish we had. Lynn deserved one. I guess sometimes we don't get what we deserve. Sometimes that's a blessing, other times a curse. But we learned about sheep hunting and we saw the wildest country left in the lower 48. And we came out of it with the feeling that we had been part of a larger whole. We had seen and been part of a wilderness that is nearly gone from this continent. We had been touched by the spirit of the land in the silence of Sheep Heaven and the banshee wind of Goat Flat and the aquamarine depths of Downs Lake and the tumbling music of the Downs Fork. And we would never be the same again.

Late at night, far from the campgrounds and highways, far from your job and your family and life in the late twentieth century, you lie in your sleeping bag, with the backbone of the Wind River Range beneath you, and you think. You think about the day you had today, and the day you'll have tomorrow when you rise, stiff and sore. You think about the mountain and the sheep and you think about why you're there.

I was there for Lynn. He's probably as good a friend as I'll ever have. In fact, I probably don't deserve a friend as good as him. He's loyal to the death, understanding of others, kind to a fault and a fabulous camp cook. He's got a bigger heart than any man I ever knew. He loves his family, his church, hunting and practicing medicine — probably in that order. He looked like a bum over there on his side of the tent, snoring through his patchy beard. But he had busted his wallet and his heart to be on this sheep hunt, and I was proud to be with him.

Portions of this essay appeared in the October 1997 issue of Wyoming Wildlife magazine.

Chapter 6

Requiem

I once knew a river, a beautiful green band that ran free from the Wind Rivers to the Colorado. She is dead now, dammed, and damned to become another generation of kilowatts for iPhones and Apple watches, another testimony to one of the immutable laws of the West: We always seek to destroy that which we cannot control. It's not easy for me to talk about her death.

This is the river of my memories, the thin ribbon of life flowing through dry sagebrush country and the deep sandstone chasms of southwestern Wyoming. The Seedskadee-Agie...Ashley's

Green River – Andy Roosa

river... Powell's river... Gasson's river. I feel lucky to have seen her through the eyes of a child before she died. I remember how she smelled, how she looked and how she felt in much the same way that I remember the sound of my grandmother's voice—difficult to describe, but impossible to forget.

My home water is born in the high country of western Wyoming, but it moves quickly out of the mountains, picking up small streams as it goes—Rock Creek, Gypsum Creek, Tosi Creek, clear beautiful little streams tumbling over granite, through spruce and fir. Along its way, it becomes the river that Bridger trapped, now in the national forest that bears his name. Ol' Gabe would be pleased, I think, to know that the Green still runs clear and free beneath Square Top Mountain. The river changes character as it moves out of the mountains. By the time Big Sandy comes in, the Green is a desert river, and it remains so until it joins the great Colorado hundreds of miles below.

I remember the smell of dry cottonwood leaves as I sat with my back against one of these timeless old trees up above the Big Island bridge. It was late afternoon on a warm November day long ago, and I was waiting for my dad. He was slipping up on a bunch of Canada geese, hugging the ground, moving slowly and silently so as not to disturb them. The old Model 12 was in his hand. My job was to stay put until he came back for me, and I did fairly well at it for what seemed like hours. It's hard, perilously hard for a six-year-old boy to sit still for very long, and as the sun sank lower, I began to grow anxious. It was getting cold, and I wanted my dad and I wanted to go back to the truck, and I was hungry, and I didn't want to be there anymore. I knew better than to strike out on my own, so I just hunkered up against that big old rough-barked giant of a tree and waited it out.

Just as the aloneness got to be too much and the tears began to leak out despite my best efforts to hold them back, I heard the shotgun speak once, twice, three times and the excitement of the hunt pushed the fear out of my mind. I waited in the shelter of the old cottonwood until I saw Gus coming back with a brace of honkers. We sat beneath the old tree and picked the feathers from those geese as the sun set. My fears forgotten, I reveled in the joy of being with my dad on another adventure on the Green. I probably wasn't much help at picking geese, but I don't remember him complaining.

I remember the petroglyphs on the wall of a rim above the river down near the Utah border. I couldn't take you to them now. The memories have faded, and I only remember that you had to take a little two-track road off the highway someplace north of the Henry's Fork, then get out and walk half a mile or so to the rim. They were on the southwest side of the rim, and it's a wonder that hundreds of years of wind-driven sand, infrequent gully-washer rains and the rigors of the desert climate hadn't wiped them out long before. No matter now, I guess they're underwater anyway.

There were figures of men and elk and bighorn sheep and those peculiar swirls and stylized shapes that nobody understands. I don't remember how the old man knew about them. Maybe one of his old desert rat buddies told him or maybe he found them on one of his ramblings after arrowheads or sage grouse. In any case, he took me to see them several times and took care to explain them to me and to tell me a bit about the people who made them. The last time we went, he took photographs of them so he would have a record of them. He explained to me that the new reservoir would cover them forever and he thought it was important that someone remember their existence. The photos he took are in a drawer someplace, but their memory will live with me forever.

I remember the night they killed the fish. With the coming of Flaming Gorge Dam and its reservoir, the suckers and carp and other "trash fish" (including the humpback chubs and pikeminnows that had been there for millions of years and would later go on to become unlikely celebrities as endangered species) had to be killed off to make room for a trout fishery. They dumped rotenone in the river at dozens of locations from Kendall Bridge to Sheep Creek and lifted the limit on how many fish you could keep. For a couple of days, we were all hunter-gatherers again, and the sound of fish flapping out their death throes echoed through the river bottoms. I don't remember why we had to be out there at night; maybe it had to do with the timing of the rotenone release, but I remember that there was a big full moon and a million stars in the sky as we parked the old pickup just below Alkali Creek. My mom stayed in the truck – she was having none of this foolishness. The old man and I set off into the darkness with his big flashlight, wearing waders and carrying dip nets, frog gigs and other tools of the harvest. No one had much experience with this sort of thing, so the equipment issue was somewhat uncertain.

We splashed around happily for a couple of hours with the moonlight shining on the water, gathering up dying fish. You could hear them flapping long before you could see them. The chemical had paralyzed their breathing, and they were dying by the thousands. It never occurred to us that we were hearing the river dying with them.

We spent less time on the river after the dam was finished and the lake began to fill. I don't think the old man ever harbored any feelings of bitterness about the loss of his river. He was a businessman and a believer in progress just like most of his friends. Maybe he simply acknowledged the inevitability of change and went on about his life. Maybe the thought of opposing change was simply too much to ask from us at that point. But I know he was never interested in buying a boat and spending weekends trolling for rainbows above his beloved and newly drowned canyons. He spoke disparagingly of the fish caught from the reservoir, saying that they tasted muddy to him, and we began spending more time in the Wind Rivers. I think he found himself in the position of finding a part of his life forever changed. Once they took the freedom out of his river, it was no longer his river.

After my dad was gone, I took to the river again. I suppose it was only natural. After all, there were still fish to be caught in the spring and summer and ducks and geese to be hunted in the fall and bobcats to be trapped in the winter. I was a young predator and I hunted and fished to live—not from a physical point of view, but from a psychological one. The river still had enough of the old magic left to satisfy me. As long as I came home with plenty of immobile critters in the back of the truck, I was happy. You could still fish or hunt from Slate Creek to Scotts Bottom with the illusion of being on the river in the old days. There was plenty of room and not very many people and you could fool yourself into believing it was all right.

It was all right, in a relative sense. We did well fishing in the early spring between Fontenelle Reservoir and the Big Sandy. There were big rainbows and bigger browns in the deep holes. If you knew what to throw at them in that cold gray period that passes for spring in the desert, you could catch them. It was a good sport for teenage boys – cold, windy, miserable, and incredibly exciting. We could almost catch a limit of fish before numb fingers and blue lips would force us to a huge cottonwood fire and some well scorched hot dogs, pulverized potato chips and other staples of adolescent males in the late 1960s. It wasn't exactly Huckleberry Finn I suppose, but it was precious to me. Even today, despite my best efforts to maintain a diet consistent with a man of my maturity, I love the smell of cottonwood-burned hot dogs and the feel of a fire on my face.

Even better, there were ducks and geese on the river in those days. We knew where they would be at various stages of ice-up, and we were the scourge of the river from the time elk season ended until New Year's. We knew every little road up and down the river and every sheltered backwater and island where the birds would seek food and open water. With my old golden retriever in the back of the truck, we'd head up the river in the early morning and start hitting every bottom from Owl's Nest to Big Island and beyond. By late afternoon, we would have reached the best of the best—the tailwater just below Fontenelle Dam where warm water kept the river open until the very coldest part of the winter. Hundreds of ducks and, if we were lucky, even some geese would pile up in this short stretch of river.

We knew every cut bank, every willow patch, and every other bit of cover that would allow us an undetected approach. If everything was just right, we could belly up silently to within just a few yards of them, with anticipation screaming inside every fiber of our souls. Then in a flurry of surprise and alarm, they would erupt into the air with a sound like thunder, and we'd bring the day to a heart-stopping climax. Intoxicated with the spirit of youth, I thought it was my river still. But there came a day when I realized that it was not my river anymore.

It came after I'd been gone for a few years. I came back to find the spirit of the river. Somehow, the country was smaller now. There were fences and locked gates where there had been none in the past. The air wasn't as clean, and you couldn't see the Uintas, the Wind Rivers and the Wyoming Range all from the same spot anymore. There were power lines and pipelines and scars from impromptu hill climbs on every rim. The river itself had changed. The fishing was better than ever before, but there were trucks with out-of-state plates parked everywhere I wanted to fish. The ducks and geese were staying away from the river by that time, and the hunting wasn't near what it had been. I watched one erstwhile duck hunter sitting in his pickup parked in the cottonwoods below Slate Creek with the engine running, the sound system blasting Eminem. He was sitting there blowing his duck call and gazing hopefully at the sky. I went home saddened by the state of things on the Green.

It took me a while to realize that I could not blame the loss of my river on the natural gas boom. It was convenient for a while – I could pass it off by blaming it on all those new folks who moved in and didn't love the country like I did. But some of them did. Some of them loved the country with the same white-hot passion that I had, that Gus had before me. When I realized that I couldn't blame it on them, it slowly dawned on me that she was mostly gone by the time they arrived on the scene. Her fate was probably sealed from the time Major Powell left Expedition Island. She screamed in agony when they closed the diversion tunnel and water met concrete for the first time at Flaming Gorge. The cottonwoods on Fontenelle creek up by the old Stepp place died quietly, with great dignity, when they drowned in the waters of a reservoir built only to prove that it could be done. The Green runs free only below the dams that incarcerate it now. But it still runs to the ocean.

There are those who love big lakes and powerful boats, fish finders and downriggers as much as I loved that river. There are those who will remind me of the economic importance of those caravans of SUVs towing drift boats pouring out of Denver and Salt Lake City, leaving their greenbacks in my hometown and buying the licenses that fund conservation in the 21st century. I salute you. I am glad you can find happiness in the way things are now. But I struggle to do the same.

Like Aldo Leopold, who once remarked that there were those who could live without wild things and wild places and those who could not, I am slow to share your happiness.

They say a person cannot visit the same river twice, that when they return it is a different river and they are a different person. So it is with my river. I am no longer young, and she is no longer wild. But she is still my home water, the river of my youth and the river of my dreams.

Portions of this essay appeared in the May 1991 issue of Wyoming Wildlife magazine.

Chapter 7

Gus

He was a natural born son of the sagebrush sea. My dad was born in Green River, WY at 6:30 PM on September 30, 1913. He was the son of Walter Fredrick Gasson and Harriet Heward Gasson, their first child. His father was 38 when he was born, his mother was 33. He was named for his much-beloved uncle Henry Franklin, the husband of his aunt Ida Gasson Franklin. His baby book records gifts that were products of his time — a buggy robe, 2 white petticoats and a white dress. It also records that his first outing was on November 15, 1913, when "Grandma took him downtown," and that his first laugh was on January 10, 1914. His baby photos show a happy, round-headed little boy in a white christening dress.

He came into the family at a wonderful time. His father was a successful "stockman" — a sheep rancher with herds that summered on the Hams Fork Divide and wintered near Green River. His mother had given up her job as a teacher when she married, and Walter built her a home below Castle Rock in Green River. The pictures of Franklin (no one ever called him Henry) as a toddler show him looking more than a little grubby at the ranch on Craven Creek, north of Opal and posing on a donkey at the Big Island bridge upstream from Green River. His was a prosperous family, and he was greatly loved. This little boy was to be the heir of a successful ranching operation and the posterity of the Gasson line.

But Franklin wasn't yet seven years old when the influenza pandemic that had devastated the entire United States claimed his father. Walt was only 44 on January 13, 1920, when he died from pneumonia brought on by influenza. Harrie was devastated, having been married for less than 9 years. A photo from that time shows Franklin, a sad-

Gus – Gasson Family Archives

eyed boy in a sailor suit, perched on Uncle Henry's lap.

But he and his sister were the apples of Uncle Henry and Aunt Ida's eyes, and they were treated like the children that Henry and Ida never had. They rode the mountains and deserts of southwestern Wyoming, and they learned to hunt and fish and cook in a dutch oven. They were close to their Gasson family in Green River, and to their Heward family in Evanston. By the time Franklin was in high school, he was a handsome and muscular young man who played basketball and football. He appears in one photo in his football uniform, now answering to the nickname "Gus" that would stay with him for the rest of his life.

Gus graduated from Green River High School in May 1933 — the heart of the Great Depression in this little railroad town — and his senior picture shows a dashing young man with a square jaw and a confident smile. He was undoubtedly confident that Ida would pay for college at the University of Wyoming in Laramie. She did, but only for so long. He pledged the Sigma Nu fraternity and spent more time than she thought appropriate drinking beer with his fraternity brothers. He dressed well and wanted to be a paleontologist or maybe a geologist. This persisted for three years. Ida told him he needed to straighten up and major in business or she wouldn't continue to pay for college. He probably thought she was bluffing. He should have known better. Ida never bluffed, and soon Gus was back in Green River looking for work.

Work came at the Green River Mercantile. The Merc was an old-fashioned mercantile store, owned in part by Henry and Ida, that carried everything from ladies' wear to horseshoe nails. Gus started at the bottom, a self-described "flunky." He joined the Wyoming National Guard in 1939. It was a fateful decision. By September 1940, his outfit (along with other National Guard Units from Washington, Oregon, Idaho, Montana and North Dakota) had been inducted into federal service as part of the 41st Infantry Division and were sent to Ft. Lewis Washington. They remained at Fort Lewis until March 1942 when they shipped out for the South Pacific. Like many other WWII veterans, Gus seldom talked about his experiences in New Guinea and the Philippines. They were not pleasant memories.

There's only one surviving photo of him from the war years. He's wearing skivvy shorts and a fatigue cap. You can see the beach and the surf in the background. On the back, it says "somewhere in the South Pacific." His muscular chest and shoulders have melted away, and the 180 pounds he listed on his induction papers has shrunk to maybe 140 tops. But the most striking thing about the photo is his face. There's no emotion of any kind there. The eyes are dead, and you don't want to know what they've seen.

Gus mustered out in the spring of 1945 and was home by VJ Day on August 15 of that year. But his war was far from over. It raged on in his head and in his heart. He came back home a mess. He had malaria and every parasite imaginable. He had jungle rot on his feet. He had what we would now call post-traumatic stress disorder. As a result, he drank. He drank way too much and way too often. Finally, his mother told him she'd have him committed to the state hospital in Evanston if he didn't straighten out. Like her sister-in-law Ida, Harrie never bluffed. He quit cold turkey and never took another drink. But the nightmares stayed with him. It took years for him to find peace in his dreams.

Soon he was working at the Merc again and had risen to the position of manager in the grocery department. T.E. Rogers was his boss, and he liked and respected Gus. The respect went both ways. He never referred to T.E. as anything but "Mr. Rogers." His friends from childhood were also involved in businesses or worked on the railroad. He was hunting and fishing again. He killed a 6-point bull elk in the Gros Ventre in 1945 or 1946 that hangs at the home place on Big Sandy to this day. He told the story of jumping three mule deer bucks on the east side of Wyoming Peak that were so big that he thought they were elk and passed up shooting at them. He hunted ducks and geese on the Green River and fished everywhere he could. He went to Ocean Lake with Ida in the winter and ice fished for burbot. He fished the Wind Rivers from East Fork down to Lander Creek. Hunting and fishing brought him more peace than any other part of his life.

Gus was by nature a man who loved learning. When he stopped drinking with his buddies in Green River, he began to read more. In fact, he read books by the dozens. So he came to the library. And he became reacquainted with Grace Gravelle. Her mother Mabel was a friend of Ida's, and Gus and Grace knew one another in passing as two unmarried people in a small town must. In time, it seemed, he came to the library only during her shift. And in even more time, they began to date. They shared a love of good books, classical music, and good food. Nearly all their friends were married, and both must have heard some biological or social clock ticking in the background. At a New Year's Eve party in 1950, they prepared the food, and something clicked. The following summer, he proposed in a canyon near Salt Lake City. She took a while to accept, still not sure she was ready to surrender her independence and her reputation as a career woman. But his gruff exterior hid a warm heart and a great capacity for love. She accepted.

He and Grace were married on June 19, 1951, at St. John's Episcopal Church—her church. In his post-war photos, he seldom looks happy. But his wedding photos are an exception. He's still handsome, with a receding hairline, and he looks absolutely overjoyed. They went to Canada on their honeymoon and came home to live in the house Aunt Minnie Hammond had left Grace at 127 East 2nd North in Green River, with the Nomis family to the west and the Viox family to the east. It was a small frame house, perfect for a couple just starting out. Gus was happy. Peace had come at last.

Their marriage was happy, too. But it struggled to bear fruit. Grace had repeated miscarriages. She carried a little girl to full term in July 1953, then lost her at birth. Another full-term baby was born in July 1954, a big healthy boy. I was named Walter Franklin Gasson, after my father and his father. No father was ever prouder of his manchild than my father was of me. From the outset, it was clear to him that this boy would be raised as a gentleman. He would hunt and fish and play football and go to the University of Wyoming like his father. He would like exotic foods like raw oysters and pickled herring like his father. He would read good books and love Wyoming history like his father. More miscarriages followed my birth, and in time it became clear that there would be no more children. We would be a family of three.

It didn't take long for Gus to realize that his wife was never going to share his passion for the outdoors if he did not put a roof over her head when she was there. She didn't care for camping, and camping with a young son was certainly not her cup of tea. So, in partnership with Aunt Carol and Uncle Grant Morck, they bought Grant and Dorothy Twitchell's lot with a foundation on it on South Temple Creek in the Big Sandy Openings. They hired the Williams brothers who ran a small sawmill on Muddy Ridge to build it, and old Bill Williams to do the fireplace. They worked alongside the hired craftsmen to build a 20'x30' log cabin built from logs cut and milled nearby. The rose quartz from South Pass was hand-picked and hauled in Gus' old green 1954 Chevy pickup. The river rocks for the chimney came from Big Sandy and were hand-quarried the same way. He loved building the cabin. In fact, Gus loved everything about the cabin. It was his place, his refuge. We were there every weekend from Memorial Day in the spring to whenever the snow ran us out in November. We had the party of all parties there on Labor Day weekend in 1961—the housewarming shindig for the cabin.

We divided up the weekends and vacation weeks in the summer so that Carol and Grant could have their fair share. Gus liked July because the fishing was better. Carol liked August because the mosquitoes weren't as bad. Someone had to be in Green River to care for his mother. I only heard him argue with his sister once, and it was about caring for their mother. There's no doubt that Aunt Carol and Uncle Grant carried the lion's share of that responsibility. In late August and early September, hunting started. First sage grouse, then elk. He only hunted antelope, grudgingly, when I got old enough to badger him into it. Deer hunting came in October, along with more elk hunting that might stretch into November. After that, it was ducks and geese on the Green River until January. As winter wore on, he'd trap a few coyotes and bobcats and then begin pacing the cage, waiting for spring when he could go to the cabin again.

It wouldn't be fair to say that all his attention was on hunting and fishing, though they were his first loves. But he had other loves, as well. He loved classical music and had a very good baritone voice. He loved books, especially those about archeology and anthropology. He taught himself to be a competent botanist and mycologist and taught me plants and mushrooms along the way. He loved Wyoming history and was an active member of the Sweetwater County Historical Society. He loved God and served on the vestry of St. John's Episcopal Church—the church he converted to when he and my mom were married. He loved horses and dogs, and there were always some of each in his life. But most of all he loved us—his family.

It was as idyllic a life as could have been possible in Green River, Wyoming in that time. In the spring of 1967, Gus ran for a seat on the City Council. He was 53 years old, a respected businessman who now managed the Merc in its entirety. He was well-educated, a veteran and a good family man. He ran for city council. The campaign flyers for

H. F. "Gus" Gasson call attention to his native birth, his college education and his role as a bank director and property owner. We went to Aunt Carol and Uncle Grant's house after dinner on election night, May 9 and stayed late. We stopped by the city hall on the way home to check on the results. He'd won, and we were all proud of him.

But in the morning, he was dead. In the early hours of May 10, 1967, he felt bad, but thought it was a case of indigestion. It didn't go away. In fact, it got worse, and he awakened my mom. She called the doctor. I vaguely remember seeing lights on and hearing voices, but I slept the sleep of a 12-year-old boy and the next thing I knew, my mom was in my room telling me that he was gone. Later that morning, friends and family gathered at Aunt Carol and Uncle Grant's house. When we got there, my dad's best friend Luke Gerdes was standing out in the driveway talking with Uncle Grant. When I walked up to him, I could see big salty tears running down Luke's weather-beaten face. I couldn't have been more surprised. Luke was the original tough guy, and I never dreamed he could cry, much less that he would.

The days that followed are a blur to me. I remember thinking that I might have to quit school and go to work to support my mom and me. I remember the funeral at St. John's, and I remember crying when I was walking out. His friend John Kalivas grabbed me and told me sternly to get myself together and be a man. I think I did, but it took a long time. We buried him in a cold spring snowstorm, there in the Gasson family plot in the Riverview Cemetery next to his infant daughter and his beloved Aunt Ida.

We had only a short time together, old Gus and I. But we were cut of the same cloth, the sons of men who had ridden horseback from Hams Fork to Vermillion Creek. Like old Walt before us and like big Fred Gasson before him, we were at home and at peace in the mountains and deserts of western Wyoming. Our love of the wild things and wild places bound us together. It brought him peace in the aftermath of his war, and it brought me purpose in the aftermath of his death.

Thanks, Dad.

Chapter 8

Cutthroats

There are images seared forever in my memory. Pictures going back six decades come to me unannounced, like the unexpected sight of an old friend. So it will be with the first Yellowstone cutthroat trout I saw above the mouth of Atlantic Creek. The light was almost gone as we rode the trail on the north side of the river just above Hawk's Rest. We spooked the fish from under an overhanging bank and it shot diagonally upstream in water just deep enough to hide it. No sound, not even a whisper in the summer twilight. And then, in less time than it takes to tell it, the fish was gone and darkness closed softly around us as we rode into camp on the Yellowstone.

So many places, so many fish, each the fish of a lifetime. Great, slab-sided Bonneville cutts on the Bear River, slowly finning, barely moving in the deep hole below a cutbank. Fine-spotted Snake River

Cutthroat trout – Andy Roosa

cutts that don't daintily sip a tiny dry fly, as status symbol fish are supposed to do, but instead charge a big weighted sculpin at full tilt and smash it headlong. Tiny Colorado River cutts in the early morning light, frost still on the grass at the Tri-Basin Divide. So many perfect places, so many perfect fish. And so many perfect memories.

Everyone, or at least every serious angler, has a totem fish. There are entire cultures built around the salmon runs of the Pacific northwest. Steelhead, the fish of a thousand casts, have spawned (pun intended) an entire counterculture in their life and death struggle to survive in the 21st century. Pick a fish, and you can identify a group of humans who identify with it, who care about the places they live and the memories they engender. For our family, it's all about cutthroats. When our family builds a totem, a monument to our country and our family culture, you can be sure that there will be a cutthroat trout there.

Wyoming has four subspecies of cutthroat trout: Colorado River cutthroats, Bonneville cutthroats, Yellowstone cutthroats and Snake River cutthroats. We've fished for all of them, and some of us have caught all of them, an achievement referred to as a "Cutt-Slam." You catch them, take a photo to document the catch and turn in a form with the pertinent information to the Wyoming Game and Fish Department. They send you a nice certificate that you can display to commemorate the achievement. But there is more, oh so much more.

For us, it all started with Dillon. Years ago, at the ripe old age of about seven, he announced at a family dinner, "Hey Grandpa, I want to catch a cutt-slam!" I was surprised he knew about it, but only a grandpa without a soul would ever discourage such an idea, so I was in. When Connor saw that this was obviously going to be a thing, he was in. These two cousins have been buddies pretty much since birth, and they have done almost everything together. Our first cutt-slam adventure started in the summer of 2010. The guys were eight years old.

It was, as most things are with our tribe, a family affair. Uncle Mark drove all the way up from Arizona pulling a camper trailer to our base camp at the Tri-Basin Divide in the Wyoming Range. This is the best of all possible campsites for the erstwhile cutt-slammer, since you can catch three of your four cutthroats with a minimum of driving time. Or so we thought. James and the boys and I came over from the cabin at Big Sandy. It was a trip down memory lane for me, and I could tell them stories pretty much nonstop from Big Sandy to the head of Labarge Creek:

"Back in the day, when the country was full of mule deer — maybe the early 1960's — old Gus and I came through here in November one time when the mule deer migration was in full swing. There were almost two hundred deer on that ridge."

"This used to be Reed Thomas' place. When I was a little kid, we used to come and hunt sage grouse here. I can still remember the excitement when we'd flush them. They seemed as big as eagles."

"This is where Joe Morris and I used to camp when we were in high school. One time we drank from the creek here, then drove up it a little way and saw there was a dead sheep in it. We figured we'd die that night, but we didn't."

"Sandhill cranes in the meadow there. Stop the truck. Listen! Aldo Leopold said that they sounded like something from the Pleistocene. What do you think?"

On and on, some stories that are funny and some that are just cool to think about if you're an eight-year-old boy off on an adventure with the men of your family. Characters that they never knew live on in Grandpa's stories. The time Uncle Grant stepped in a deep hole over on Blucher Creek, and he went clean out of sight and his hat went floating off toward the Sweetwater. The time Grandma and Grandpa got stuck and had to walk out in the middle of the night and the dog got into a porcupine. Elk hunting stories, arrowhead hunting stories, stories about our family and our country, the legends of living and the living legends of Gassonistan on the upper Green River.

They were like little coyote pups, just taking it all in, with eyes wide and shining like silver dollars when we rolled into Uncle Mark's camp on the little creek below the three-way divide. I've always loved that place, the beginning of the Green, the Bear and the Snake. Depending on where any given snowflake might fall in December (or for that matter, July) it might give birth to a droplet of water that ended up in the Colorado, the Columbia or the Great Salt Lake. Labarge Meadows, the birthplace of my own natal waters, would be our first stop in the morning.

It was the bright, shiny morning of what was to be a very long day. We had dined like kings in the camp of the boys' beloved great-uncle. Boneless spareribs and spuds in the evening, fresh breakfast burritos in the early light of dawn. The little guys didn't eat much. They were too excited to get on the water. I did, because old Gus had taught me long ago that an army—including an army of anglers—travels on its stomach. Soon, we were off.

In early July, there's still frost on the grass in the morning at the head of Labarge Creek. But the boys were ready for anything. Well, mostly ready for anything. Dillon's boots had been left back at the cabin. Still, he gamely continued and walked off into the morning sunshine wearing his Crocs. We were on the water early that day. But the fish seemed to be missing. Labarge Creek is managed specifically for Colorado River cutthroats, and a multi-year program to eliminate the non-native fish had been successful. But the cutthroats were few and far between. In fact, they were completely absent. We worked hard all morning, prospecting each likely looking hole and carefully slipping up on fish we knew must be there. They were not.

When we stopped for lunch, it was obvious that adjustments needed to be made. The big guys were surprised, the little guys were openly disappointed. We had one very small Colorado cutthroat to show for some very long hours. It was time for decisive action. We would abandon the Green River drainage and head up and over into the Greys River. With some lunch on board and a new plan, optimism rose again in the ranks. After all, fishermen—even junior-sized fishermen—are inveterate optimists. We were off again. We had a plan.

It's about 64 miles from the Tri-Basin Divide to the mouth of the Greys River, near Alpine, Wyoming. It isn't paved. Sometimes it's graded, sometimes it's not. It's a long way on a hot afternoon with young anglers who are increasingly tired and dispirited. We'd stop for a while and fish this likely looking stretch of water. Nothing. Get back in the truck and drive. Repeat. Repeat. Repeat. By late afternoon, the boys were done in. I had one ace in the hole, and it came just in time. Not every tributary of the Greys River is created equal, and this one had always been good to me. It was our last chance. We needed to pull a rabbit out of a hat here. Fortunately, the magic was still there.

I stopped at the first good deep hole with a riffle above it. We would have only a few minutes to fish before we ran out of both daylight and good will. It was becoming drudgery for the little guys. They weren't smiling anymore. They were just toughing it out. I'd like to say it was on the first cast. It wasn't. it might have been the third or fourth for Dillon. All of a sudden, in the long-shadow light of that late afternoon in July, the water was churning and he was hollering for the net. I was the net man on this one, and I prayed nothing went wrong. It felt like it took hours for him to bring the fish in, but he did it. I netted it on the first shot and suddenly everything was different. We were catching fish!

In no time at all, Connor had a fish in the riffles above the bend and we were on our way. We had Snake River cutts. We celebrated with dinner in Alpine. We all ate like wolves, and we talked about the trip back to camp. The thought of replaying the long trip up the Greys didn't sound good to anyone. So we dug out the maps and came up with Plan B. We'd drive south the length of Star Valley to the Smith's Fork Road and go back that way. It was a long way, but most of it was paved and we wouldn't be reminded of the day's painful and mostly fruitless fishing. We were off.

I love Star Valley. It's every bit as beautiful as Jackson Hole, and you don't have to shoo the hedge fund managers out of the way to drive through Afton. There are no captains of industry or World Bank billionaires to clutter your view of one of the West's most beautiful landscapes. South through Alpine, Etna, Thayne, and Afton in the evening light. The smell of first cutting hay. Cranes in the meadows. Sundown as we begin to travel on the gravel at the foot of Salt River Pass. Only 22 miles of gravel this way, and we were ready to be back in camp. Dark now and counting down the miles as we went. Then somewhere around mile 19, the headlights of the big Ford diesel caught the snowdrift up ahead. What? This cannot be! We're only 3 or 4 miles from camp, and it's 9 PM. We're tired. We've been up since 5 this morning! Maybe if we get a run at it....

Upon closer inspection, we found that the drift was between four and five feet deep at maximum, and the unmistakable signs of the fools who had bet their future on high clearance and momentum were plain to see. We were within walking distance of camp, but it was dark and wet, and we had two young guys who were way beyond tired. They were exhausted. We tucked our tails between our legs and headed back the way we came. Back to the highway. Trade drivers. Back through Star Valley. Trade drivers again. Back up the seemingly endless Greys River road. We arrived in camp at the stroke of 2 AM. I felt, as old Gus would have said, like I'd been rode hard and put up wet.

We weren't up at the crack of dawn. The boys slept in. The men slept in. We ate breakfast. We took showers. We planned the day with the care that Eisenhower took with Normandy. We would drop down far below our camp. We went all the way to the national forest boundary before we even tried to fish for the elusive Colorado River cutts. But at the crack of 10 AM, bingo! Connor had one, then Dillon had one. We were halfway to a cutt-slam now. Morale surged, and when I asked them if they wanted to head for camp or take a long drive in search of Bonneville cutts, they were ready for adventure.

So off we went. Down the creek to the highway. Down the highway to the other highway. Lunch in the truck as we drove. Naps. Change drivers. More naps. Around the horn of the Wyoming Range and over onto the Bear River. It was mid-afternoon by the time we got to Cokeville, but we were determined to make good on this one. We were experienced cutthroat fishermen now, and we would settle for no less than success. The family honor was at stake.

They say that when Brigham Young sent the first colonists from Utah to the Bear River country, there were big fluvial Bonneville cutts in the river that weighed in excess of 30 pounds. Heaven only knows how old a fish that big might have been. I'd like to have seen one. They didn't last long. The settlers took them by whatever means they could to feed themselves. They dammed the tributaries. They diverted the water for irrigation. It was a microcosm of the entire interior west. If humans could do something that was bad for these fish, they did it. Not with malice aforethought, but they did it. By the time my family came on the scene in the late 1800s, the best fishing was long gone.

But the cutthroats hung on. My grandfather caught them in the first decade of the 20th century in the stream we would fish this very afternoon. And exactly a century later, these fish were thriving again. We would find no giant fish lurking in the mainstem Bear River, but we would find fish. Thanks to the work of two generations of fisheries managers, land management agencies, private landowners and conservation organizations like Trout Unlimited, these Bonnevilles came back from the brink of disaster. These Great Basin fish, once nearly extirpated from the upper Bear River, were thriving.

It was a long, rough road into our favorite spot, the same spot old Walt fished in 1909. It was late afternoon when we got there, and the shadows were growing long. We worked hard for an hour before we found them. It was a pod of fish, all about the same size, holding in a deep hole in a bend below some willows. They were good fish, really good ones for our young anglers. All we had to do was figure out what was on the menu. This was the hardest fishing the little guys had encountered. These fish were completely ignoring anything on the surface, and they were in 3-4 feet of clear water. It required a precise cast, a fast sink, and the patience of Job. But if we had to stay all night and into tomorrow, we would figure out how to catch these fish. As it turned out, all it took was a little weight and more than a little persistence. In rapid succession, Connor scored first and then Dillion. Just as the sun was setting, we had them—two gorgeous cutthroats, each just a shade over 20" long. The boys were over the moon.

We came out in the dark, and we had convenience store pizza and soda for a very late dinner, but no one cared. It was still two hours to camp, but no one cared. We were all pretty much exhausted, but no one cared. We felt like kings, like conquering heroes. We had met the challenge; we had fought the good fight and had the photos to prove it. We were men of all ages, but we were men who could fish.

CUTTHROATS

On the road to the home place the next morning, my mind was in other places. All the other places we wouldn't have fished if we hadn't been after these three specific fish. I was replaying all the conversations we wouldn't have had if we hadn't been in those perfect places in pursuit of those perfect fish. I was thinking about how our family had been doing this in our country for so long, and how these places and these fish had changed us.

It wasn't about fishing, or at least not all about fishing. It was about our family, our country, and our water. It was about Wyoming and love and life. It was perfect.

Chapter 9

Haystacks Elegy

The old man in the little store at Red Desert, Wyoming, had a bighorn sheep skull he'd picked up in the breaks south of Man and Boy Butte back in the '50s—the 1950s. Both the man and the sheep skull looked like they could have just as easily found one another in the 1850s. Both were sun-dried and weathered relics in this little oasis in the middle of the sagebrush sea. The country south of Wamsutter was still wild when my dad and I used to stop in at the store for a Coke on our way home from a day trip to Fort LaClede or the Haystacks. The old man and the little store grew older and shabbier together over the years as the Lincoln Highway was replaced by

Red Desert – Andy Roosa

HAYSTACKS ELEGY

Interstate 80. Finally, they both passed away. I wonder whatever became of that sheep skull.

I wonder whatever became of the country he found it in, too. I tried to take my grandson and his dad there a while back. The sagebrush sea was gone, chopped up into little pieces by a spider web of roads and pipelines, well pads and compressor stations. It took me three hours to find the old road along the north side of the Haystacks, and another hour to find the little two-track that dead-ends where we used to camp. The old timers claim that Butch Cassidy used to camp for a day or two in the Haystacks too, back in the day. He could rest his horses and watch his back trail to make sure nobody was following him on the Outlaw Trail from Hole in the Wall to Brown's Park. It was a dry and lonely camp then, but not anymore. It's part of one of the largest gas fields in America.

We can stand on the same rock pile that a bighorn sheep stood on once, quick draw the smartphones out of our pockets and call our cousins in Los Angeles or Las Vegas or Lost Springs. We can open Google Earth and know exactly where we are. There's no app to tell us exactly where we're going, but I think I know. I think we're going to a place where nobody knows, and nobody cares about bighorn sheep or Butch Cassidy or the Haystacks. We're going to a place where as long as we've got a smartphone, a soccer field and an SUV, we could care less about the Flat Tops or Man and Boy Butte or Fort LaClede. We're going to the place where comfort lives and freedom dies. Welcome to the 21st century, fellow travelers.

In the great Western novel *Lonesome Dove*, author Larry McMurtry's two protagonists, Woodrow Call and Augustus McCrae go into San Antonio to find a cook to replace the one who has quit, having had more than enough of their quixotic cattle drive from Texas to Montana. They are surprised at what they find. In their days as young Texas Rangers, San Antone was a wild place. But now it's become like every other town, with too many people and too little of the old excitement. Gus says, "We'll be the Indians if we last another 20 years. The way this place is settling up, it'll be nothing but churches and dry-goods stores before you know it. Next thing you know, they'll have to round up us old rowdies and stick us on a reservation to keep us from scaring the ladies." As I drove from one well pad to another, trying to figure out where we are by checking the legal descriptions on the locations, I think I know how he felt. There are trucks going full bore in every direction, but not a soul here knows or cares where our camp was back 30 years ago. None of them know or care about the old man or the store or the sage grouse and deer we used to hunt here. I think perhaps my time and my place here in this part of Wyoming is gone.

Maybe Gus McRae was right. Maybe they ought to just round us up, us old rowdies who were here long ago. They could load us up on a little bus every so often and take us out to fish in the park or maybe to a baseball game. That way we wouldn't have time to sit and think about what we've lost. We wouldn't be frightening the politicians or the oil companies with our talk of what once was, what might have been and what still could be. But like Woodrow Call, I doubt that's going to happen. I suspect we'll keep right on doing what we're doing now, and old men like me and the cowboy poet Wally McRae will be left with the thoughts he expresses so well in his poem "Things of Intrinsic Worth":

> *Great God, how we're doin'! We're rollin' in dough,*
> *As they tear and they ravage The Earth.*
> *And nobody knows... or nobody cares...*
> *About things of intrinsic worth.*

Maybe that's just it. Maybe 21st century America cannot be expected to recognize things of intrinsic worth—things that are essential to us as human beings. Or maybe we can't be expected to agree on what those things of intrinsic worth really are. It's long been my observation that the people of my own state are often quick to sell our birthright for a mess of pottage, like Esau in the Book of Genesis. Maybe we're unable to recognize that places like the Pinedale Anticline or the Haystacks are indeed our birthright. If you don't see the beauty or feel the connection to those places, you're pretty unlikely to view them as a birthright.

The history of the interior West suggests that it's much easier for people to form a connection to high mountain country with snow-capped peaks and burbling streams than it is for them to connect with rocks and sagebrush. When Theodore Roosevelt and Gifford Pinchot created the national forest system and sent their "forest arrangers" out to draw the lines on the maps, they mostly left the sagebrush country alone. Likewise, when the Wilderness Act gave another generation of mapmakers a chance to protect the wild qualities of some places, nearly all of them ended up in the high country. There have been (and remain) areas in the sagebrush sea that were designated Wilderness Study Areas. They've been so designated for an entire generation, with little or no action to determine their fate. No connection, no protection.

So how to foster that connection, that sense of stewardship? In the polarized political climate of the times, doing it by federal edict seems completely impossible. Likewise, at least in my state, leading with a green/climate change-related problem statement is undoubtedly doomed to fail. If there is to be broad acceptance of the need for protecting crucial wildlife habitats, migration routes and other important features on the landscape, it has to be driven by science and developed by a broad coalition of people who have a stake in the outcome. The sage grouse working groups developed in Wyoming to guide decisions for managing sage grouse habitat might provide a model. Of course, it's important to note that those groups died a swift political death as soon as their critics found a friendly ear in a new administration.

One thing is certain: We cannot continue to view these places with a frontier mentality that treats them as ripe for exploitation. Since 1890, that mentality has guided Wyoming's approach to sagebrush country. One could say it has guided America's approach to that ecosystem. Until well into the 20th century, those yellow squares on the map that identify lands managed by the Bureau of Land Management were simply "the public domain"—lands that belonged to everyone and as such, lands that belonged to no one. Until relatively recently, the notion of stewardship—active efforts to preserve the integrity of these lands and right the many wrongs that have been perpetrated on them—has been limited. That cannot continue if we intend to pass them on to future generations.

The challenges are many and the political will is probably not there. It will take a Herculean effort that involves government, non-profits and the private sector to change the trajectory out there on the ground. It will take some compromise—a foul word in the lexicon of the ideologues on all sides of this challenge. But I'm optimistic enough to believe that it can be done. I believe we're smart enough to identify big chunks of the sagebrush sea that can be excluded from energy development—fossil fuel or renewable. I believe we're wise enough to keep cows and sheep on the land in a balance with the long-term health of the range. I also believe we're wise enough to know that we've metaphorically ridden feral horses into a box canyon from which there is no escape. We cannot continue to allow feral horse numbers to grow unchecked, despite our best efforts within the current legal structure. A lot of things will have to change if my grandchildren are to be able to have the experiences that have blessed my life and the lives of so many others. But we can and must do this.

I was reminded of that recently when my grandson and I were out in a small desert mountain range looking for an elk. It was a blustery day, with a wicked west wind and drifted snow. We were the only ones in the country, and we'd run out of elk tracks when we stopped on a rim overlooking a vast monochrome landscape of gray and white. We glassed for the wapiti for a while, then just stood there in the cold and the wind to take it all in. We just stopped hunting for a moment and looked. It was that best time of day, before the sun is full up and the clouds are all pearly gray and pink on the horizon. The wind was blowing a gale as sharp as a knife. It was bitter cold. There wasn't much stirring, but it was a grand time to be out and to just take it all in. Not a lot of people might pause to look at the sky when the air temperature is 10 degrees and the windchill is minus 13, but I guess that's why there aren't very many of us here in Wyoming. It looked like something Charlie Russell might have painted.

HAYSTACKS ELEGY

I've always loved the art of Charles Marion Russell. Nobody ever captured the feel of the high plains and sagebrush country like Kid Russell. He could paint horses so realistic they seemed to jump right out at you when you looked at them. And he always got the light just right, like someone who had actually spent time in the saddle, not just in the studio. And Ol' Charlie, he knew how to paint the sky.

Even the most dyed-in-the-wool-and-Carhartt Wyomingite forgets to stop and look up around every so often. We never stop to think about how breathtakingly beautiful it all is. It's not like we don't appreciate the beauty of living where the sky stretches from this horizon to that one and where you can feel the strength of the earth beneath your feet. We wouldn't live here if we didn't appreciate it. But sometimes we forget to enjoy it.

A few years ago, we lived in Maryland for a while. We were temporary residents of a small town about 70 miles west of Washington, DC while I worked there. It was a nice place in many ways. But you could never see the sky. It was usually cloudy or at least hazy, and the woods made you feel closed in after a while. It was claustrophobic, but nobody there even noticed. I'm not sure we did either for a while. But one night we went to a movie in Frederick — *The Horse Whisperer*. You know, the one that's loosely based on Buck Brannaman, where the girl and the horse get hurt and the mom hauls them both to Montana to heal them. When they get to Montana, there's a big, panoramic shot of the Rocky Mountain Front leaping up out of the plains and a sky so big it just knocks you back in your seat. My wife and daughter saw that shot and immediately both burst into tears. They were ready to strike out for home that night because they missed the enormity of the Wyoming sky.

I think most of the people in the world never get to have that experience — to be struck dumb and stopped dead in their tracks by the enormity of the sky above and the earth below. They rise too late to see that pearly gray and purple horizon before the sun hits the country on a cold day like Connor and I did. They're too busy at work to look up and watch as the clouds roll from horizon to horizon on a summer afternoon. And they're stuck inside their iPhone waiting for their kids at soccer practice when the fall sunset turns the whole world to gold. They live their whole lives without ever looking up.

Maybe that's a good thing to think about when we contemplate these vast and empty lands of the sagebrush country. Maybe we ought to vow that this year, no matter what, we're going to take time to look up and see the sky. We're going to stop long enough to feel the connection between earth below and God above. We're going to take a minute to realize where we are and why we're here. And we're going to be thankful for the sagebrush sea and the Charlie Russell sky.

Portions of this essay appeared in the February 2013 issue of Wyoming Rural Electric News.

Chapter 10

Grace

My mom was born on January 27, 1919, in Rock Springs, Wyoming. Her family lived in Green River, 15 miles west. Green River was a rough and dusty town, a railroad town, fueled by coal from Rock Springs and the hard work of good people from all over the world.

Her entry into this world was not an easy one. Her father, George Gideon Gravelle, had passed away three months before during the great influenza epidemic of 1918, and her mother was devastated. Mabel Rumble Gravelle was a 37-year-old stay-at-home mom with two other children to care for and no income to support them. A new baby so soon after the loss of her husband was a shock. She struggled to bond with the little girl, but soon gave up and refused to even feed her. But the women of St. John's Episcopal Church came to the rescue, caring for the little family until Mabel could do it on her own.

Grace grew up, the baby of that little family, in a small frame house right on the main street just across from the courthouse. Her sister Mareese (12 years older) and her brother Gail (9 years older) doted on her. She had a wonderful extended family that she loved and who loved her. She often said it wasn't until many years later that she realized that her family had been poor. She never felt poor, she only felt loved.

To us, her early years seem like a story from another century—after all, they are. Their little home had four small rooms—a living room, a kitchen, a bedroom, and a bathroom. It was heated with coal burned in a big cookstove in the kitchen and a smaller parlor stove in the living room. Washing was done in large copper

Grace – Gasson Family Archives

boilers heated on the cookstove. Foods were kept cold in an icebox, with a large block of ice on top, and a pan below to catch the water as it melted. The family never had a car, but they had a Bible. It sat on the library table in the living room, and it was from this Bible that my mother gained her earliest lessons in the faith that would sustain her throughout her life.

She was baptized as an infant and confirmed as a teenager in St. John's Episcopal Church in Green River. It was a cornerstone of her life. It was her home church, and it was hard to tell who supported whom to the greater degree — did the church sustain my mom or did my mom sustain the church? It's hard to say, but they were inseparable for nine decades.

She roller skated, played jacks, marbles, and hide-and-seek with the other kids. She was happy doing that, but she was just as happy playing alone or reading. Though she grew up on one of the great rivers of the American West, she never learned to swim. Her teenage years came during the deepest part of the Great Depression. Those were hard times, with many people in Green River out of work and hoboes by the score riding the Union Pacific rails in search of a future. But it was hard to be any poorer than the Gravelles were already, so their life simply went on. In fact, the Depression gave rise to my mom's life work. When she was a junior in high school, a government assistance program called the National Youth Administration offered employment to teenagers. Her high school superintendent Mr. McIntosh and the county librarian Mrs. Joslin, knowing of the family's dire situation and my mom's love of books, got her a job in the library. She loved it from the first day.

She graduated the salutatorian of her class and was offered an academic scholarship to the University of Wyoming. But she was the sole breadwinner in her family by this time, her older siblings married and gone, and $50.00 a month was too good to pass up. She stayed at the library. Never a social butterfly, she didn't date until she was out of high school and didn't enjoy it much then. Her life was the library, and she loved it. She saved her money, took an occasional vacation to Denver or Salt Lake City with her mother, and quietly resigned herself to a single life.

When the war years came in the 1940s, the troop trains thundered across the desert and stopped in Green River for coal and water. The GIs took their doughnuts and coffee from the Red Cross, took themselves to the bars for a drink, and some of them in desperation even found their way to the Sweetwater County Library. But none of them ever found my mom — or at least never found their way into her heart. She gave that heart only to the library, and in time rose to be the head librarian for the Sweetwater County library system. She was, in the language of the time, a "career woman" and she believed she would always be the same.

In fact, it wasn't until much later, after the war — after all the GIs who were going to come home had come home — that something changed. Franklin Gasson — "Gus" — who was five years her senior, had come back from the war in the South Pacific a mess. He had malaria. He had jungle rot. He had what we would now call post-traumatic stress disorder. But he read books, and he came to the library. One thing led to another and soon they were dating. Green River was a small town, and these two were well known by pretty much everyone. I'd like to have heard the grist from the rumor mill in our little town about then. But gossip aside, they had a great deal in common, and they had found love in an unlikely place. He bought a green '49 Desoto that had a fold-down back seat big enough to sleep on. "For camping," he explained. Her mother was scandalized, but she seemed unfazed.

Gus was a quiet guy who carried a lot of scars from the war. He put on a gruff exterior, but she found him to be unfailingly kind, gentle and loving. He was wonderful to her mother. And he loved the mountains and desert country of southwestern Wyoming with all his heart. When he asked her to marry him, she didn't hesitate. They were married at noon on June 19, 1951, in the little church she had attended all her life. They went to Canada on their honeymoon. They fell in love with a painting they saw in Helena, Montana on the way north and scrimped and saved the entire trip so they could buy it on their return. He promised her a steak dinner in Jackson, but when they got there, they found that the painting had wiped the budget clean, so they split a hamburger instead.

It was a good marriage, especially for two people who had few other prospects, and my mom was a wonderful companion for my dad. They had been raised about as differently as two people in a small Wyoming town could be raised, but they loved one another completely. Neither was particularly demonstrative about that affection. We've always joked that when my mom passed, her epitaph would read "Yes, I'm dead but I didn't want to say anything." She wasn't much for saying anything, but she was wildly emotional and talkative beyond belief compared to my dad.

As real as their love was, it struggled to bear fruit. My sister Gail Renée died at birth in 1953. I came along a year later, a big, healthy baby and they were overjoyed. My mom was 35, my dad was 40. I was the only child they would have. She seldom told the story of hearing me praying for a little brother or sister when I was three or four years old. I told her that I didn't think that God heard my prayers, and I wanted her to pray for a baby, too. She explained that God had plans for us that we didn't understand. She must have grieved mightily over their inability to have more children, and she never spoke of it.

We lived in a small frame house that had belonged to my mom's Aunt Minnie. She had left it to my mom in her will, and Mom had managed it as a rental unit until my dad and I came into her life. She loved that house. It had a large yard and a garden, a front porch with a swing, and it was only a block away from her mother and her sister. She knew everyone in the neighborhood, and they knew her. She could leave me out in the yard, faithfully guarded by our springer spaniel Curly, and bottle peaches or do the laundry on the old Maytag wringer washer on the back porch and listen to the radio — KVRS in Rock Springs.

I suspect it wasn't always easy for my mom to be the only female in our home. My father and I were born with a love of the outdoors. She was not. She didn't like cooking over a fire. She didn't care to sleep on the ground, and she certainly didn't care to hunt. She fished, probably out of self-defense in the beginning. But I remember her being a tolerably good angler, though prone to fits of emotion with a fish on. I was there when she caught the biggest fish of her life, using one of the most unorthodox techniques I've ever seen. She set the hook on the big rainbow, turned around and ran up the bank and all the way to the truck. I can still see that big fish bouncing through the sagebrush....

In time, my dad realized that if they were to enjoy the outdoors together, he would have to put a roof over her head. In partnership with my aunt and uncle, they built a cabin. My mom loved it from the beginning. Nearly every weekend between May and October and every family vacation was spent there. We rode horses and hiked and fished and picked mushrooms and wildflowers. We did it all together, and it made us the family we were. In truth, it made my mom the woman she was. Even into her eighties, my mom loved going to the home place.

When I was in second grade, my mom went back to work at the

library. In the summer, I had a babysitter. During the school year, I came home to an empty house, and she came home as soon after school as she could. I hated it, but it served its purpose. Again, my mom worked her way up through the ranks and before long, she was the head librarian again.

The years passed. They seem idyllic now, though I doubt that they were quite as perfect at the time. Home, church, family, work, the cabin—the fabric of my mom's life was centered on us. It always was. She was a wonderful mother to a boy growing up in the best of all possible worlds.

Then, unexpectedly, it all came crashing down around her ears. In May of 1967, my dad ran for city council. Late on the night of the election, we stopped by City Hall and learned that he had won. My mom and I were incredibly proud of him. I think he was proud too, but he would never have admitted it. We went to bed happy. In the morning, he was dead. Coronary heart disease—we had no idea. He was only 53. It was as though our world had collapsed in on us. My mom was devastated. I was crushed. It was a nightmare.

As she got older and could talk about it more, she told the story of feeling utterly without life. She couldn't come to grips with the loss of my dad. She prayed for days for help and strength. There were no answers. Just before the funeral service, she prayed again. But this time she heard a voice. She said she never knew if it was my dad's voice or God's, but it was a voice, and it said, "It's all right. I am here." Suddenly, all the things she had professed to believe for 48 years became real, and she could go on. And go on she did. Each day, waking up alone, without a husband. Each day, being a mother to an angry young man who blamed the world for taking his father. Each day, earning a living to support our little family and holding us together. My mom was a hero, as sure as I stand here today, my mom was a hero.

Never did I need a hero in my life as much as I did when I learned that I was going to become a father when I was still in high school. Kim had come into my life when she was a senior and I was a junior. We fell hard for one another. Then she left Green River the day after she graduated, not yet knowing she was pregnant. So began the hardest time of our lives. It was obvious to everyone involved that keeping this baby wasn't a great option. We chose to place the child for adoption through a church social services agency. Looking back, it was awful. They packed Kim off to Salt Lake City, while I stayed in Green River to finish high school. And when she reached her due date, they put her under general anesthesia and induced labor. The baby was long gone to the adoptive parents before she ever woke up. We knew he was a boy, and that was it. The pain of that loss would be with us for decades.

The next few years were hard. Sometimes, they were hell. But my mom stuck with us. She believed in us, both as individuals and as a couple. Her love for us and her faith in God kept her going and she got us through. And when we were married after our first year of college, I suspect that Mom realized that Kim had a better chance of helping me to be something other than a menace to society than she did. If she had any regrets about "losing" me, she kept them to herself and always treated Kim with great love and respect. We lived with her during the summer, and I think my mom loved having another woman in the house. Many years later, she came to live with us. I suspect Kim liked having another woman in the house, too. It was touching, in her last few years, to see my sweetheart return that love as she cared for my mom.

During the years between those two events, my mom completed the greatest professional achievement of her life, overseeing the construction of a new library in Green River to replace the one that had been in service since 1906. I don't think I ever really knew my mom as a librarian, or the leader of a team of librarians in multiple libraries in several communities, or the overseer of a major construction project. She left work at work. But I do know that libraries don't name rooms for people very often, and there's a Grace Gasson Room in the library in Rock Springs. I think she retired feeling proud of a career spent helping people love information and learning as much as she did.

When our daughters came along, my mom was more than ready to be a grandma. She was there to help out with each of them when we came home from the hospital. She loved those three little girls with all her heart. She bathed them, played with them, and read stories with them for as long as they liked. They stayed with her when Kim and I needed some time to ourselves. And they loved being at Grammy's house. She had an entire assortment of different breakfast cereals—not just one, like at home. She had an entire credenza full of Good Housekeeping and Reader's Digest magazines and an unlimited supply of library books. She didn't have many chores that needed done, and she didn't care if you just sat and read. For Jenny, Beth, and Sarah, it was heaven.

Somehow, the years went by faster and faster as those three little girls grew up and became women. They graduated from high school, and Grammy was there. They went off to college, and Grammy was there. They got married, they graduated from college, they had babies—and Grammy was there. She was steady and constant, never complaining, never asking for much of anything, just there. She was gracious. She was Grace.

In time, the old house in Green River became too much for her. An automobile accident in 1986, a knee replacement some years later, and the steady march of time made it hard for her to keep living on her own. When we suggested that she move to Cheyenne with us, she was again gracious. She tried it for a few months, decided she liked it and came back to stay. Our family moved her lock, stock, barrel and 700-pound pieces of petrified wood to Cheyenne.

In retrospect, I don't think it was ever home. She had lived for 80 years in the same town in which she grew up. Her friends at age 80 were the same friends she had at age 8. But she loved being with her family, so she began a new life in Cheyenne. She went to St. Mark's Episcopal Church. She joined a new PEO chapter. She did some volunteer work. But it wasn't home. She stayed because she knew it was the right thing to do, and because she loved us.

In the end, with her worldly possessions reduced to those which would fit first in an assisted living apartment, and later in a nursing home room, she seemed to care less and less about those things. She cared about us. Even when she couldn't remember the names of her grandsons-in-law or her great-grandchildren, she loved them. She loved all of us. Right up to the end, she loved us. And right up to the end, she was gracious. She was Grace.

Chapter 11

Farewell

The outcome was inevitable. You knew exactly how her story would end. It wouldn't be easy. They never are, and this one would be harder than most. She was the dog that brought us back to having dogs again, after the last heart-breaking loss. Now she was dying, and we knew it. She knew it too, and she had lived in pain long enough. For all three of us, it was not about the what anymore. It was about the how. And one thing was for sure: we would do this together. This beloved old dog would not die alone or scared or in a strange place. She would die with us, unafraid and knowing that she was loved.

She came to us in 2008, already a middle-aged dog. She was a project, a rescue dog from our friends at the W9. She was in pretty bad shape, and she'd been through a rough time. She was thin and ragged looking, with a dull brownish coat. She was afraid of pretty much everything, especially men. We weren't really sure we had room in our life for a dog anymore, but we couldn't say no. She hired on with our outfit a few days short of her 8th birthday.

She was Kim's dog from the start. They learned to go for a run together every morning. It wasn't easy. Missy didn't understand what was expected of her at first. We even had to call in an expert to teach us to redirect her attention, so she didn't go berserk every time she saw another dog or a person or a rabbit. But she was intelligent, and she wanted to please, so in time she came around. As the weeks went by, she learned quickly. And she morphed into an amazing dog. The dull brown coat all blew out and she was as shiny and black as a piece of obsidian. And just about as hard—she had muscles on top of muscles everywhere, as she settled into a high-quality diet and daily exercise.

FAREWELL

Missy – Gasson Family Archives

At 75 pounds and 0 percent body fat, she could lope forever. And sometimes she did.

It was easy to see from the beginning that she would never hunt, even in our family of hunters. Her bloodline was great, but too much troubled water had passed under the bridge, and she was terrified of any loud, sudden noise. Gunfire, fireworks and thunderstorms were her demons. So, we put away the notion that we had a hunter and loved her for who she was — sweet, strong, and happy. She fit in our outfit like she'd been born here.

That winter, when Kim's running moved indoors to the treadmill, Missy and I moved outdoors to the school section west of our place. She'd retrieve a tennis ball no matter how far I threw it, no matter how many times I threw it, no matter how deep it was buried in the snow. Lots of times, it was pitch dark when we'd go out in the morning and she'd disappear into the void in her perfect black ops camo, then reappear spectral a few seconds later with the snowy tennis ball clutched in her mouth. We became buddies that winter. We will always be buddies.

She's happy today. She was up early and ready to be fed. She's insistent about meals these days, not because she's hungry but because she's figured out that the pain pills come with the dog food. She keeps trying to move mealtime up earlier and earlier. It's not about the food, it's about the pain management.

So, we go outside, and she totters around the north pasture a bit to take care of her business. She doesn't like to walk outside much anymore because the footing is uneven, and she stumbles and sometimes falls. She's thin as a snake, weak and teetery. If she was bipedal, she'd be using a walker. But we go very slowly and she manages. She likes the concrete driveway—there's nothing to trip over. I brush her and a cloud of hair goes sailing off into the breeze. She's blowing her dry, brittle coat like crazy.

We come inside and I feed her—canned dog food now because her teeth are just about gone, and she has a tumor about half the size of a tennis ball under her tongue. Her tongue lolls out to the side because it has nowhere else to go. It breaks my heart to watch her eat, but I hide the Tramadol inside a chunk of dog food and she gets it down. Within minutes she's resting quietly.

Later, she watches from the office window as Kim and Jora the border collie go for a run. Three years ago, she was there. Chasing a cottontail, following a fox track. Not now. She watches them disappear in the distance. Another heartbreak. So, we sit together and talk about the old days when she felt good. She doesn't feel good anymore, except when she can sleep.

Last night, Kim laid down beside her on her bed and just snuggled her. She's always trusted Kim. She relaxed and fell asleep. I hope that's the way it goes when the vet comes tomorrow afternoon. I had hoped she would pass that way on her own, maybe even go when we were at the cabin. But that's not going to happen. She clings to life like she's afraid to move on. Maybe we all do, to one degree or another, when our time comes.

I couldn't talk about it yesterday. It's hard to do it now, but at least it's over. The world's best family vet has come and gone. So has Missy's last day with us. She and Kim and I shared a shady spot in the backyard. We sat and talked with her and petted her as Gary shaved a little spot on her foreleg. Then he gave her a quick injection in that leg and in a few seconds she was gone. No fear, no pain, not even a little surprise. She just quietly died. He left, and we just stayed there with her for a while. I don't think we knew anything else to do. We just sat there and cried for a while together.

Then we picked her body up, so thin and bony, wasted by her illness. We carried her to the grave we had prepared for her out in the east pasture. It's getting to be a little crowded back there, with Molly the springer spaniel and Dinah and Cat and now Missy. Maybe that's one way to grade the level of meaning in your life — the number of animals who loved you unconditionally and who you grieved over and buried in your pasture. We gently arranged her body on her bed — in the same position she used when she slept on it. We said a prayer. Then very slowly, very gently we covered her with the soil of her home. We replaced the buffalo grass and blue grama and flax in a low mound that will slowly even out over the fall and winter. By next summer, it will be shortgrass prairie again and her body will return to the land she loved.

But her memory will live on. Her long, loping stride when she was in her prime. Her gentle dark brown eyes. Her love for a good ear rub. Her embarrassment at public displays of affection from cats. She was a kind, sweet, gentle soul who came into our lives and loved us unconditionally. She never judged us, she learned to trust us. She waited every day for just a little bit of our time — a run, a few throws of the tennis ball, her breakfast or dinner. She was meek and kind and humble. She was what we all wish we could be. She loved as we all wish we could love.

And her spirit will live on. If you were to ask, "Do you think you'll see her again?" I'd probably answer flippantly that no one as ornery and prideful and mean-spirited as I am should ever be allowed to sully the afterlife of a great dog like that. But what I'd really be thinking is that God would never have given us a dog like that if He thought that we'd only have a few years with her. What I know in my heart is that she'll be there when we get there, and she'll be strong and fast and full of life and happy to see us again.

Most of the important things in life aren't easy. Birth, death, love — all are hard, terribly hard sometimes. The very foundations of our lives are built of hard things, as they should be. Foundations, if they are to be foundations, must be hard to be strong. You blessed our lives in so many ways, old dog. God be with you 'til we meet again. We love you.

Portions of this essay appeared in the March 2016 issue of Wyoming Rural Electric News magazine.

Chapter 12

Bison bison

I wish I could have seen them. They say there were more than 60 million wild bison in North America prior to 1800. There were plains bison—the smaller of the two American subspecies—from what is now the panhandle of Florida to northern California, from Coahuila to central Alberta. They were the economic and cultural center of native culture. And they were the victims of a genocide conceived to exterminate that culture. All of what is now Wyoming was the land of the plains bison. They evolved here, and the grasslands and sagebrush country of my home evolved with them. By 1900 only 300 of them remained.

There are about 15,000 free-ranging bison now. Hemmed in by the 21st century, they make a living on little islands of habitat in places like Yellowstone, the Henry Mountains in Utah, and other scraps of prairie in the Great Plains and the interior West. They are an anachronism, these inbred little showcase herds that exist in little pockets of what made America what it was in the time of Thomas Jefferson. The good news is that their extinction is unlikely. The bad news is that they are unlikely to ever be what they once were. I wish I could have seen them then. But I'm blessed to have had the opportunity to see a shadow of them—the enduring legacy of wild, free-ranging bison right here in Wyoming. I have been close enough to feel the thunder of their hooves in the sagebrush and smell their musk in the autumn sun. I have been a bison hunter.

They say the hardest part about hunting a bison in Wyoming is drawing the tag. I'm not sure that's true. Bison hunting is about as hard as you want to make it, and I wanted my bison hunt to be a strictly ethical, fair, and reverent experience that was as true to the spirit of these magnificent animals as it could be. There would be no sitting at the salt lick on the National Elk Refuge when the snow drives them to the valley floor in Jackson Hole. We would do it the hard way. We would hunt them in the mountains, in the aspen stands and conifers and sagebrush where they spend their summers. We would keep an eye out for grizzlies because we are not the top link on the food chain. And if we killed a bull, we would butcher it and pack it out on horses or mules, the way it should be done. This would be a once in a lifetime experience for me, and if that made it harder, so be it.

But it wouldn't be a solo experience. I had a team to back me up. Steve was the key player, the first-round draft choice. Probably one of the best field biologists I've ever known, he knew these bison and their habitat like no one else. In addition, he had been involved in many backcountry bison hunts and delighted in using his horses and mules on those hunts. Jill was another field biologist and all-star player. She was working on the challenges surrounding disease, habitat, and elk feed grounds in the area. That meant that she had a good feel for where the bison were at pretty much any time in the year. Mark 1 is my brother-in-law, my partner in so many outdoor adventures. We've hunted and fished together for decades, and he would never miss an adventure like this. Mark 2 is a talented outdoor writer and photographer, just the guy you want to capture the images of a hunt you'll only do once. We made a great team.

I spent some time in the area in late September—my favorite time of the year in Wyoming. Jill told me she'd been seeing bulls in a spot on the national forest, but close to the boundary with Grand Teton National Park. That was good news and bad—good to know there were bulls in the area, bad that they might walk across the line into the national park and be off limits to us. So, I went to see. Sure enough, there were three bulls in a prescribed burn that Steve had worked on a couple of years before. All three were big bulls, but one was simply huge.

Bull bison have a presence, an attitude. It's not aggressive unless something gets them stirred up. They are simply unafraid of anything. Not people, not grizzlies or wolves—not anything in their world. They look at you somewhat balefully. Or maybe they just look right through you. In any case, they just go on doing what they're doing as if you don't exist. You are less than insignificant to them, maybe bordering on nonexistent. I guess if you weigh 2,500 pounds and can run fast and jump high, fear just isn't much of a thing in your life. This trio of big boys hardly even glanced in my direction. I gave them plenty of room.

The heart of fall came quick enough, and I was ready. I had all the gear, including enough coolers to hold a boned-out bull bison. I had multiple knives and sharpening equipment. I had the rifle of choice—after trying multiple great rifles, both my own and those offered by friends—I settled on Mark 1's Browning BAR in .300 Winchester Magnum. It was heavy, but that wasn't a problem. The important thing was that it was extremely accurate and packed a heavy punch. The notion of wounding any animal is unacceptable. The notion of wounding an animal who can then stomp you into a greasy spot in the sagebrush is doubly so. I drove to Jackson to meet my beloved brother-in-law.

I've never been able to sleep well the night before a big hunt. I'm like a kid on Christmas Eve. Mark 1 and I shared a hotel room, and I'm sure I must have kept him awake with my tossing and turning. It felt like morning would never come. We had originally planned to leave at 6:00 AM, but Mark 2 suggested a later start to make sure that the light was good for photos. It was the longest 60 minutes of the year. With a quick stop for fuel for both the crew and the trucks, we were headed north. Steve was in the lead, pulling the horse trailer with the two mules. Jill rode with Mark 1 and Mark 2 rode with me. We saw a big bull near the highway—off limits to us since he was in Grand Teton National Park. We headed east toward Togwotee Pass, then south on a forest system road. It's a washboard-rough gravel road, and we took our time.

We found a good spot to park the trailer and unload the mules. Silas and Bugs are old hands at this, and they're great mules. Bugs is a dun-colored mule that Steve loves to ride. Silas is coal black and built like a brick outhouse. They knew the drill and stood quietly as we saddled them and gathered our gear. Then the two Marks and Jill and I drove a small two track a mile or so and waited for Steve to come up with the mules. He wasn't far behind. The plan was to walk the two-track to the national park boundary, then turn north through a prescribed burn where Jill and I had both seen bulls in the past.

Mark 1 and I walked in the lead, with the three Jacksonites and the mules not far behind. We walked about a quarter mile when the trail turned abruptly north at the park boundary. We stayed on the trail for only a few hundred yards when we topped a little ridge and I saw him. He was in a dense aspen stand, about 300 yards away (308 to be exact—Mark 1 checked him in the rangefinder). Steve looked him over carefully and told me he looked old and that he had broken the tip off his left horn, probably in a fight with another bull.

I looked at him again, facing away from us and toward the morning sun. He was huge, so big that he looked out of place, like a mastodon or some other relic of Pleistocene megafauna. He was black, like a hole in space, absorbing all sunlight. We watched him for a minute or two, then eased up quietly another hundred yards or so along the edge of the old burn to the lip of a deep draw. I knew that the light breeze was at our backs, blowing our scent right to him, but if we could make the other side of the draw, I'd have an easy shot. Jill was careful to warn us that some bison hunters had been charged by bulls and that we should be careful. I thanked her for reminding us of our fragile mortality and we set out.

The two Marks and I dropped down into the draw on a game trail and began climbing up the other side. Steve and Jill held the mules and watched as the bull caught a whiff of us and instantly whipped around to face us. He couldn't see us, but he knew we were there. I stopped two or three times as we climbed up out of the draw, so I'd be steady and ready to shoot when we got to the rim. Mark 2 was to my left a few yards, already taking photos. Mark 1 was slightly to my right and immediately behind me. A few yards short of the rim, I sank to my knees and then to my belly to begin the final approach, slow and quiet. When I lifted my head to look up through the sagebrush, the bull was staring directly at me. Not just in my direction, but right into my eyes. He knew exactly where I was long before I could see him. Mark 1 checked the distance and whispered, "52 yards" then repeated it in case I hadn't heard him. I watched the bull in the scope, crosshairs fixed on his immense forehead and waited for him to turn enough to expose his neck. It felt like forever, but it was probably no more than two or three minutes. Finally, he seemed to relax a bit and turned to the right. I quickly picked a spot about six inches behind that broken left horn and squeezed the trigger.

The rifle must have roared. It generates a terrific muzzle blast when you turn it loose, but I have no memory of the sound. My attention was focused on the bull, who crashed to the earth as if some invisible cable had simultaneously jerked all four legs out from under him. I was prepared to follow up that first shot with three more if needed, but it was clearly unnecessary. He was dead.

Remembering Jill's warning, I approached him very carefully in case he tried to rise. He didn't.

It was then that I began to get a little shaky. The sheer size of him was daunting, no question about it. But it was more than that. Size alone does not convey power. I have a friend who owns a Clydesdale that weighs over 2,000 pounds, but he's as gentle as a lamb. This guy was over a ton also, but there was nothing gentle about him. He was built like a tank, and the broken horn and numerous scars the whole length of him testified to his ferocious capabilities. His power came from within, a fierce vitality this old bull had carried with him for many years. His was a greatness of spirit that cannot be expressed in physical terms, a spiritual quality that made the taking of his life both very sad and a little overwhelming. The two Marks stood back politely while I knelt by the bull, put a hand on his shoulder and gave thanks to God for him and for this day.

When I rose, we all shook hands and congratulations were offered all around. Steve and Jill brought up the mules and showed them the bull so his smell wouldn't spook them. Mark 2 took dozens of pictures. I was glad. I didn't want one moment of this to be forgotten. Not because I wanted to record my conquering of this bull, because I could not and did not ever conquer him. I took his life, and his body would feed my friends and family. But his spirit would live on unconquerable in the sagebrush and the aspens. It would be in the Tetons and in Spread Creek and the Buffalo Fork. It would be with the spirits of the wolves and the grizzlies and the elk. And a little piece of his spirit would be within me forever.

We took lots of photos in an effort to capture a little of that spirit, then we settled into the work at hand. Jill and I went back to the trucks to gather up knives and a saw and all the other necessary gear. By the time we got back, the boys had made a fine start on skinning the right side. He had fallen on his left side, with his back up against a small aspen. It became obvious in short order that we would have to get him away from the tree to skin him and bone out the meat.

Steve mounted Bugs and we tied a rope to the bull's leg. He got Bugs in position, took a dally around the saddle horn and touched the mule with his spurs. Bugs charged forward and hit the end of that rope like a brick wall. The dead bull never even quivered, didn't move an inch. Steve lined out the mule for a re-ride and hit it again. Nothing. Again. Nothing. Mark 2 boarded Silas and we tried both mules pulling in tandem. Nothing. It was like the old bull was rooted to the earth itself. You might as well try to drag the Grand Teton to Nebraska as try to move this bull.

On the final try, the rope broke and slapped Silas across the butt. The big black mule went bucking and crow-hopping off through the sagebrush. Cowboys say that most mules can't buck hard enough to throw off a saddle pad, much less a decent rider. But it sure looked to me like Silas was doing a fine job of it. With each successive jump, Mark 2 caught a little more air. As Silas neared the edge of the rim, it became obvious that Mark was looking for a place to push the eject button. Then Silas launched one last spectacular effort, and our erstwhile bronc rider went straight up in the air like he'd been shot from a cannon. I thought for a moment that he might land on his feet, a very impressive trick and one that I hoped he would want to show us again. But he landed on his shoulder and broke a finger in the process, so I didn't press him about a re-ride.

We all gathered around the half-skinned bull and determined that maybe it would be easier to cut down the aspen than to move the bull. Mark 1 had a cordless reciprocating saw—a welcome bit of 21st century technology in this otherwise 19th century picture—and neatly cut the aspen off at ground level. We skinned the bull back to the middle of his back and started boning out that side.

Lest anyone who has not undertaken the butchering of a bison think that this is like peeling an orange, let me explain. At any given time, we had four knives in the hands of people who were experienced buffalo skinners. Steve alternated between a razor-sharp filet knife and a big combat knife. I used a series of folding hunting knives, and Jill wielded a large scalpel, changing blades as needed. Mark 2 used whatever knife came to hand. There were over a dozen knives involved, and the skinners frequently traded dull ones for sharp ones. Mark 1 sharpened knives when we needed them and skinned when we didn't. My brother-in-law is good help in an operation like this. Once we had the skin peeled back, we started boning meat and putting the pieces in big plastic bags and then putting the bags in feed sacks. Each full sack weighed about 100 pounds. Each side of the bull yielded about three sacks.

By early afternoon, we had half the bull processed and we were ready for lunch. We took a load of meat and walked the mules back to the trucks. I brought a variety of cold cuts, cheeses, bagels, chips, sodas, apples and cookies. If it's true as Napoleon said that an army travels on its stomach, then it's doubly true for a small squad of buffalo hunters. The last thing I wanted was a hungry crew. So, we ate hearty and lingered a bit over lunch. I don't think this was about any reticence about getting back to work. It was just about enjoying being in the moment and a picnic on a perfect fall day. Mark 2 reminded me that I still hadn't filled out my tag. I told him that you could take the boy out of Sweetwater County, but not vice versa and that I might want to shoot, skin and butcher two or three more bulls that day. There was near mutiny in the ranks when I mentioned this, so I tagged up.

We finally headed back across the draw and went back to work. We tried again to drag the carcass into the open, this time succeeding in moving it almost four inches. But it quickly became evident that it would be a lot easier to just get Bugs around on the back side of the bull and roll the carcass over, using his legs as levers. That worked nicely, and we began skinning the other side.

I should mention something here about bison hide. Like everything in, on or associated with a bull bison, it's big and heavy. The whole hide laid out flat measured about 8 feet by 12 feet. That part was obvious, but not so obvious was the thickness. A bison skin is no thicker than an elk hide across the rump but gets progressively thicker towards the front of the critter. It's almost an inch thick on his neck. I've never seen anything dull a knife like the hide on a bison's neck. Up there, you skin 6 or 8 inches of hide, get a sharp knife and skin another 6 or 8 inches and repeat the process until it's done.

It seemed to take longer on this side, but in about three hours we had it done. We had four more bags of meat plus the head and hide. It was late afternoon now, and we were tired. We were also very aware that any grizzly bears in the neighborhood were smelling dinner here and we didn't care to be part of the menu. Mark 1 took Jill back to her truck so she could make her softball game. Mark 2 and Steve and I stayed to get the last loads to the truck and get everything packed up. By the time we were loaded, Mark 1 was back, and the shadows were growing long. The sun was low over the Tetons and the light was warm and golden, that special hue that only exists in the fall in Wyoming.

When we got out to the main road, we helped Steve unsaddle the mules and let them roll and cool off a bit. Then we loaded them and the tack into his trailer. We eased out on the main road just as it was getting dark. As we headed north toward the highway, Mark 2 told me how impressed he was with my "moment of reverence" after I killed the bull. I mumbled something about it being only good manners to give thanks after God gives you one of His creatures. It felt good to talk about this. By the time we hit the highway, the stars were out. I don't remember what we talked about, but it was a good talk with a good friend. There's something about good friends and good mules and good talk by dashboard light that makes hard work more than worthwhile.

Years have come and gone now since that night. I look at the old bull bison skull that hangs now above my left shoulder as I write, and I think of that golden day with those good friends. And on those warm days of October, when we ride or hike the wild country of Wyoming, we all feel the spirit of the bison that fed our families and our spirits that fall and evermore.

Giving thanks – Mark Gocke

Chapter 13

The Home Place

It seems to me that one of the most defining characteristics of human beings is a sense of place. We long to belong to some place. We want to feel connected to some part of this world. The great writer and historian Wallace Stegner said that this "sense of place" required at least three things: a unique geography—something that made that place special on the land, a remembered history—something that made that place special to someone, and a connection between that history and the present—something that made that place and its past important for the future.

For my family and me, that place is in southwestern Wyoming. Our roots are a mile deep there. On both sides, generations of Gassons, Gravelles, Mischlers and their connections have called the windblown sagebrush deserts and gritty little mining and ranching towns home. We've been there through the cattlemen/sheepmen wars of the late 1800s, the influenza pandemic of 1918, the Great Depression and two world wars. We've herded sheep and cattle, worked on the railroad and in the mines. We've birthed our babies and buried our dead. We belong there, and we are as much a part of the harsh landscape as it is of us. While we may have done our part to shape it in a place or two, it has done much more to shape us.

One place in that great wide open has particular significance for us. It has been our retreat for five generations. It has provided not only a sense of place, but a place of sense—a place where we could stop for a day or a weekend or a week and look at ourselves as individuals and as a family. It has offered us peace and quiet and some distance from our neighbors. But more important, it has offered us both the freedom

THE HOME PLACE

The home place – Gasson Family Archives

of the wilderness and the comforting blanket of family traditions. It has been the site of a few honeymoons, the best birthday parties, a lot of back-breaking labor, countless fishing trips and elk hunts, and some of the most memorable moments of our lives. The home place is our place.

It isn't much to look at. Put kindly, it is rustic. Put more precisely, it's primitive. This is not one of those designer cabins that you might find in Jackson or Aspen or Tahoe. It doesn't have a fancy name, like "Road's End" or "Almost Heaven." We don't have an ostentatious rustic gate. We don't have wi-fi. This is one room, twenty feet by thirty feet—no frills. We have running water, if you run to the pump out back and pump it yourself. We haul our drinking water from town and use an outhouse that dates back to the Eisenhower administration. Our furniture is composed of castoffs dating back to that same period, some of it so old that it is retro-chic again. Not that chic matters much. We've never been much on chic, but we have been on the home place.

I remember when we built the place. I was four—old enough to believe I was helping, but too young to actually help. My parents and my aunt and uncle bought it from a family friend. It was just a foundation and an acre of lodgepole pine forest under special use permit from the U.S. Forest Service. There were a few neighbors, mostly folks from Rock Springs who were looking for a weekend getaway in the mountains where they could bring their kids for some fishing and what can only be termed now as "experiential learning." We didn't call it that then—it was just "goin' to the cabin."

But we went. And we built it, or at least we helped. The technical knowledge came from those artists in logs, the Williams brothers. They ran the last of the little scab sawmills in our end of the country, located a ridge or two over from us, and they cut the logs for the cabin there. They milled them and cut them onsite, turning lodgepole pine into a cabin in one summer. With rose quartz from South Pass for the fireplace and granite river rock from the same neighborhood for the chimney, we had a small cabin built from the land on which it stood. And so it stands today, in large part unchanged.

Between that first year and now have come the memories, volumes of memories. All of us who have loved this place have our own set of cabin memories. Some are our own private memories. Most of them we share with the rest of the family. And we pass them on from one year to the next, from one generation to the next. They form the legacy of our family.

Many of my own cabin memories are somehow tied to wildlife, the products of a lifetime of fascination with wild critters and the places they live. I can recall the time Uncle Grant and I spooked a black bear out of the willows on Dutch Joe Creek. That was over sixty years ago now, but I can still see him as if it had happened yesterday. He burst out of the willow thicket breaking branches and plowing up the soft turf as he sprinted away. I don't recall being frightened, though he seems to me to have been as big as an ambulance. I remember how fast he could run, despite his rolling bulk. And I remember the way the muscles of his cinnamon-colored shoulders rippled with power and I remember the musky smell of bear in the air.

I remember the way my dad looked when he fished, standing on one of the granite boulders that rimmed Big Sandy Lake. He wore a light wool plaid shirt against the morning cool and his old battered felt hat. He seldom spoke when he was fishing, and the only sounds I recall were the whisper of the wind and the light "plop" of a Colorado spinner hitting the surface. We fished a lot in our twelve years together. I suppose that we were like fishermen everywhere — sometimes we caught a lot and sometimes we got skunked. I cannot remember how many fish we caught on any given day, but I remember how it felt to be fishing with my dad, and I would give a great deal to be able to do that just one more time.

After his death, my mom and I continued to go to the cabin. My mom was always a part of that place. Even in her eighties, she returned every summer to renew her relationship with it. She told me once that it was hard to be there for a while after the old man died. It is a tribute to the strength of my mother that her love for the place endured. But it is no great surprise. If you look through the accumulated memories of this family and its special place you will see that my mother is a part of many of them. She was there, hauling rock for the fireplace. She was there, fishing with my dad. And she was there to be a single parent to an angry young man who would rather go hunting and fishing than go to school.

During that period of time when she was struggling with unplanned widowhood, I was taken in by the family of my dad's best friend. They had bought the cabin just up the ridge from ours, and they refused to let my dad's death keep me from doing the things he and I had loved to do — like be at the cabin. I learned many things from old Luke. Two were particularly important: He taught me to work hard, and he taught me to hunt elk. Like the old man, he was a fanatic elk hunter and a student of how elk behaved in a given area under a certain set of circumstances. Like most really good elk hunters, he knew the country well, and he had a system based on weather, snow depth and experience. It was a very effective system. Someplace in my basement, there's a picture of me standing outside the cabin with my first elk — the product of Luke's system.

I can see and feel that morning as if it were yesterday. It was gray and spitting light corn snow that morning. The wind had a razor edge on it, reminding us that late October is awfully close to winter at 9,000 feet above sea level. It did the same for the elk, I guess. They were on their way to winter range that morning, and we knew they were there. Three sets of elk tracks went into that stand of timber on Jim Creek, but none came out. Larry and I were selected to "push the timber" while the others waited in strategic spots for the elk to break into the open. We moved slowly and quietly, stopping to look and listen every dozen steps or so. Never looking for a whole elk, just a piece — a nose, a leg, a rump. Moving as silently as the breeze in our faces. I hadn't walked a quarter mile when I saw her. She was the first of the three, two cows and a calf, and she was looking back over her shoulder. I stopped and waited, not daring to breathe. She walked steadily toward me, with steam coming from her nostrils at each breath. I seemed to be invisible to her, standing there absolutely still, as she came on and on. It seemed to go on for hours like this, until she stopped broadside to me at no more than fifteen yards.

I can still see myself in slow motion as Uncle Grant's old .270 came to my shoulder and I can still hear the deafening roar of the rifle in the dawn stillness. I can still remember the strange and potent mixture of exultation and sadness and the smell of blood in the snow as we dressed her and packed her back to the cabin. And there I am in that old photograph, standing beside the hanging elk quarters, with the snow falling and the cabin in the background.

The cabin remained in the background as I met Kim, went to college, and left our hometown for Laramie, Pavillion, Gillette, Cheyenne and finally Laramie. But we have always come back to the cabin. Indeed, it became the background for some of the best parts of our life together. We spent the first night of our honeymoon, out of gas in a borrowed Bronco watching the moon rise and set over the high desert on the way to the cabin. We would spend a week there together every September, hunting antelope and sage grouse on frosty mornings when the aspens were kissed with gold. We fished, or at least I did. Kim was a half-hearted angler from the beginning. If the fish weren't biting, she was happier just enjoying the country than she was at flogging the water in hopes of attracting a trout. But she was a fierce hunter of big game.

To this day, I believe she holds the family record for number of big game animals taken while commuting to and from the cabin. I have never understood this. She has never been any kind of road hunter and has always hiked her share of the mileage on all the marathon hunts we have undertaken in pursuit of elk, deer, and antelope. But for some reason, when the marathon is over and we are headed back to the cabin having packed my kill the requisite miles back to the truck, critters stand stupidly by for her.

I saw her do it twice in one day once. We decided to take a break in elk hunting to look for a deer. She had a buck license and a doe-fawn tag. We rose at the crack of ten and meandered down the road. There, standing in the lodgepoles, was a two-year-old barren doe—the perfect table deer. Kim and the deer watched each other for a while, each munching their breakfasts. Then Kim stepped off the road and dispatched her with a single neck shot. We field dressed the deer and took it back to the cabin.

After a rest and a snack, we tried to go deer hunting again. This time, we made it a little farther afield and even got to listen to a little bit of the Wyoming Cowboys football game on the radio before she spotted a four-point buck having lunch in an aspen grove. This deer was even closer, and even dumber. To this day, I swear she was completely invisible to him as she stepped off the little two-track road, bolted a cartridge in, and sent him one step closer to pot roast. She has been doing it for years that way. She was a part of the legends of the cabin from her first day there, and she remains so today.

It was only natural that our children should be a part of the cabin, and that it should be a part of them as well. Our son Clark wasn't reunited with us for a long time, so his cabin time was delayed for 46 years. But his three sisters were cabin girls from the get-go. First Jenny, followed by Beth and then Sarah. We brought Jenny there when she was only a month or so old. She went with us to pick mushrooms at the cabin before she ate solid food, and she returned with her own children in due course. So did her sisters. These girls were rocked to sleep in the big chair by the window. Each bathed in the waters of South Temple Creek and slept under the stars as the coyotes yipped in the midsummer night.

They caught their first fish there, and we recorded each one in photographs. Each of the girls shows a bit of who they are in these pictures. Jenny is quiet and holds a small brook trout delicately with a shy smile. Beth at the same age has a similar small trout, but she has a grin from ear to ear and a death grip on her fish. Sarah is taller at the same age and is wondering if the fish is a male or a female.

They were built a lot closer to the ground when we took those pictures. But they grew. They learned the names of the creeks and the peaks and how to find the North Star. They learned the stories and myths of the cabin and the country. They had adventures there and built memories of their own. Jenny was the first to bring a boyfriend, and later a husband, to the cabin. It must have been hard for him, falling into the middle of old stories and inside jokes, but he got used to us—and he and Jen built memories of their own. He has rebuilt nearly every part of the cabin at one time or another. His mark will be on the place in a literal sense for decades to come.

Beth was the first to nearly perish there. She and I made a foolhardy assault on a timberline lake in the spring only to get caught in a fierce blizzard. We were soaking wet and exhausted when we finally made it down below the snowline. But this young lady of the ready laugh and the stream of words proved to me that day that she was indeed made of tough stuff. Like her big sister, she too brought a young man to the cabin. In fact, he proposed to her there. She accepted, and their three kids have loved it as she did.

And Sarah—it seems like yesterday when I left her at the far end of another lake while I went to dry our sleeping bags in the sun. When I came back, my seven-year-old competition junkie was clutching a twenty-inch cutthroat, asking "Is this one bigger than your fish, Dad?" She spends the lion's share of her summers there now, with her family or her friends. It's her happy place.

Our son Clark represents a special case. Born to two high schoolers in the early 1970's, he was placed for adoption shortly after his entry into this world. It was a closed adoption, long on secrecy and judgment but short on compassion. It was also the hardest and most painful decision of our lives, if one of the wisest. We never saw him, never held him, never even knew what happened to him. He was simply gone, and the pain of losing him was indescribable. But through a series of events that can only be described as miraculous, he came back to us at age 46. And he came to the cabin.

With us and with their own families, they all return to the cabin. Like fish swimming upstream to their home waters, they return to their home place. And they bring with them a love for the land and an ethic for the use of that land. They grew up knowing the value of a sense of place and valuing a place that makes some sense. Like the old axe that's been the family for fifty years—only replaced the handle three times and the head twice—the home place remains a priceless part of our lives. Each generation has used it, maintaining some things, adding or subtracting others to meet their needs. But the love of the family and the love of the land have remained constant. We seem to have passed that constant on to our own children, and they have in turn passed it onto their children. It may be the most precious gift we can give them—a legacy of love.

Portions of this essay appeared in the February 1999 issue of Wyoming Wildlife magazine.

CRAVEN CREEK

www.ingramcontent.com/pod-product-compliance
Lightning Source LLC
Chambersburg PA
CBHW040300170426
43193CB00020B/2959